Dangerous Encounters – Avoiding Perilous Situations with Autism

of related interest

Breaking Autism's Barriers
A Father's Story
Bill Davis,
as told to Wendy Goldband Schunick
ISBN 1 85302 979 3

Asperger's Syndrome
A Guide for Parents and Professionals
Tony Attwood
Foreword by Lorna Wing
ISBN 1 85302 577 1

Understanding and Working with the Spectrum of Autism
An Insider's View
Wendy Lawson
Foreword by Margot Prior
ISBN 1 85302 971 8

Getting Services for Your Child on the Autism Spectrum
DeAnn Hyatt-Foley and Matthew G. Foley
Foreword by Carol Gray
ISBN 1 85302 991 2

Dangerous Encounters – Avoiding Perilous Situations with Autism

A Streetwise Guide for all Emergency Responders, Retailers, and Parents

Bill Davis
and Wendy Goldband Schunick

Jessica Kingsley Publishers
London and Philadelphia

First published in the United Kingdom in 2002
by Jessica Kingsley Publishers Ltd
116 Pentonville Road
London N1 9JB, England
and
325 Chestnut Street
Philadelphia, PA 19106, USA

www.jkp.com

Library of Congress Cataloging in Publication Data
A CIP catalog record for this book is available from the Library of Congress

British Library Cataloguing in Publication Data
A CIP catalogue record for this book is available from the British Library

ISBN 1 84310 732 5

Printed and Bound in Great Britain by
Athenaeum Press, Gateshead, Tyne and Wear

Contents

Chapter 1   What is Autism?   11

Chapter 2   Why Training is Needed   17

Chapter 3   Characteristics of Autism   23

Chapter 4   Why Law Enforcement might be Called   39

Chapter 5   How to Communicate   47

Chapter 6   Challenging Circumstances for Emergency
             Responders   63

Chapter 7   Particular Challenges for Ambulance and
             Emergency Room Workers   75

Chapter 8   Fire Rescue   83

Chapter 9   Shoplifting and Store Disturbances:
             A Special Problem for Retailers and Law
             Enforcement Officers   89

Chapter 10   How Emergency Responders and Parents
             can Work Together   95

Chapter 11   Preventing Problems in Everyday Life   115

             EPILOGUE   139

             APPENDICES   141

             INDEX   169

Thank you – my beautiful wife and daughters, my very cool and powerful son and – my colleagues Dennis Debbaudt, Doris Washington and Lenore Wossidlo – Dr Fran Warkomski, the Qualls, the Keares, Dr Penn, "Mr Mike", Shelley Reynolds, FM97, Mayor Smithgall, Chief Heim and the Lancaster City Bureau of Police

Bill Davis

To all my dear friends and family who have given me unwavering love and support. There will never be enough words…

Wendy Schunick

A Walk in the Mall

for my son

I just wanted to walk in the mall today,

I have a blueprint of this maze in my head…

I am following a picture that leads to the store with the blinking red light, it absorbs me, I like to stare at it.

It holds and comforts me –

It is warm and safe – it is the same every time. Predictability befriends me.

And I am up the moving stairs, walking past the toys.

Around the bright store, thru the loud store and I am walking – fast! Head down!

Fast!

Following my path, following my picture, turning quickly and…

Bang!

Harsh lights! Loud noise! A piercing cry!

I go back to my path – eyes darting – fingers busy – my skin is crawling and…

I find my red light and stand right up against it and it consumes me and I bathe in its warmth and…

Bang!

The noise will not let me be, it surrounds me and attacks me, and my stomach

hurts

and my head aches and throbs and the loudness is there again.

So I press my head up against my light – just let me fix myself and…

Bang!

A baby crying! Loud screaming and then…

Piercing questions – I seek pressure, I seek solace, I seek comfort and quiet and floating –

I just want my red light to turn on and off,

On and off,

On and off,

On and off,

On and off,

And I scream with anticipation and need and I wave my fingers and flap my hands and jump up and down,

up and down

up and down

up and down

up and down and…

Bang!

A man with six buttons and no face, roaring, yelling, and I turn away and…

Bang!

He comes closer and I ache now and shiver and my skin turns itchy and warm and…

Bang!

He touches my neck, and grabs my shoulders and turns me and…

I am repeating what he says again and again and,

Again and again and,

Again and again and…

Bang!

The floor is pressing me and open mouths are yelling at me, hands touching me

and

I picture my room and trains and my cards and… my dad and…

Bang!

I can't move my hands or my head and I am biting, flailing, aching, screaming, punching, eyes rolling, mind racing and flashes of light and sound have taken me and…

My dad can help, my light will help and…

I don't know what will happen next, and there is no comfort here, no understanding here and…

I just wanted to walk in the mall today.

(Bill Davis)

Chapter 1

What is Autism?

A fifteen-year-old Plano, Texas boy with autism was fatally shot by a police officer after an emergency call to a respite home. The boy, staying at the home for the weekend, became upset when a television show ended. After hollering and throwing a plastic laundry basket at a mentally retarded man, a staff member called 911. A police officer arrived and the boy and respite worker met him at the door. The boy and policeman shook hands and discussed the fact that they both had the same first name. The respite worker left the room, and the calmed boy went to the kitchen. He came back with a butter knife that the policeman believed was about to be used as a weapon against him. The officer commanded the boy to drop the knife, but after the second command he shot the boy twice to protect himself. The boy later died from chest wounds. A wrongful death suit was filed by the boy's parents.

In Harrisburg, Pennsylvania, police officers noticed a tall, black eighteen-year-old male looking in the side window of a house and acting strangely. They approached the suspect and asked what he was doing. The young man started yelling "No", and the officers tried to grab him. At that point, he tried running. The officers threw him against the house and tackled him to the ground. Hearing screams and a loud thud, a woman came out of the house yelling that he was her autistic son. After lengthy questioning the officers finally removed the handcuffs from the teen. His parents then rushed him to the emergency room where he was diagnosed with a separated shoulder. The family filed suit against the city and police officers. They are also trying to pass a law mandating autism awareness training for emergency responders.

"We're going to school," the father said to his son.

The son, who has autism, started violently throwing things around and banging his body. Then he ran over to the computer and typed, "Please take me to school. I want to go to school."

"Okay. Let's go."

The boy started punching his dad.

"But I thought you just typed that you want to go to school!"

The boy ran back to the computer and typed again, "Please take me to school! School is good. I want to learn."

"Okay. Here's your coat." With that, the son threw even more punches at his father.

What was going on here? What's the lesson to be learned? The answer: the boy's brain wanted to go to school, but the autism wouldn't let him cooperate physically. Even though he could type the words, "Take me to school," his body wouldn't listen to his brain. Why not? No one knows. The disorder is a puzzle.

My seven-year-old son, Christopher Davis, also has autism. He was a fairly normal developing toddler when at age two, symptoms started to appear. He began to lose his speech, walk on his toes, stop eating, stop sitting in a chair, stop using utensils, stop looking at us, stop hugging us, stop kissing us, and stop playing. He started eating nails, drapes, and the plaster off the walls. Chris crawled into the corner of the apartment, wouldn't set foot outside, went limp if we touched him, rocked back and forth, spun around the room, and played with his fingers fifteen hours a day.

After struggling to get a diagnosis, we began a life-long journey of hard work and constant care for our son. We set up an in-home educational and therapeutic program and an internship program for therapists with nearby F & M College. Christopher has gone from the child I described to a child who is now able to work on computer, go to the mall, swim, do gymnastics, do math, spell, read, write, and hug. He's the greatest little guy, and the hardest worker I know. We love him to death.

The Autism Society of America defines autism as a life-long neurological disorder that disrupts a child's learning and socialization. The word "autism" is derived from the Greek word for "self" because the disorder is associated with children who seem self-absorbed. People with autism are over-processed and out of sync with the world. So they have difficulty processing sounds, sights, touch, or smells. This leads to many other problems including stomach disorders, eating disorders, language disorders, and seizures.

People with autism can have many or just a few of the disorder's common characteristics. No two people exhibit the exact same symptoms, making autism a spectrum disorder. Some people can be very high functioning and others very low functioning. You may meet autistics who have PhDs and autistics who are mentally retarded and very self-injurious. A very small percentage of autistics are savants. That means they have a genius level skill, usually in art, music, or math. Some have an uncanny ability to know dates or state capitals. The thing to remember, however, is that they may be completely deficient in typical, everyday skills.

Workers in the emergency service field should be very aware of the fact that people with autism can be violent and aggressive. Teenagers, in particular, have been known to be very aggressive and have some very peculiar behaviors relating to hormones and sexuality. But understand that autism is not a psychological disorder. The peculiar behaviors you might encounter are not from a person who is out of control or has a psychological problem. It is not a result of poor parenting. His actions cannot be physically helped. All his cells, neurons, enzymes, and hormones are pushing him toward certain behaviors. You might as well forget everything you know about communicating with a typical human being because it's not going to work with autism.

Autism is the nation's third most common developmental disorder following mental retardation and cerebral palsy. The Center for Disease Control and Prevention estimates that at least one in every 500 children in the US will have the disorder. It is four times more prevalent in males than females, and has increased almost 200 per cent in the last ten years. These are epidemic proportions! In spite of such large numbers, autism is still a mysterious neurological disorder. There are no known causes or cures, and the majority of medical, educational, and service professionals are unfamiliar with it. Some people think the cause of autism is environmental, meaning it could be from vaccinations, antibiotics, or drugs given during pregnancy. Nobody seems to know for sure. It is said that there will never be a cure for autism there will be many cures.

Chapter 2

Why Training is Needed

One early hot summer evening my son, Chris, and I were sitting on the sofa watching TV with the front door left ajar to get a breeze. When I answered the telephone I turned and noticed he was no longer sitting with me. So I said to the person on the phone, "Gee, my son's not on the sofa. Let me just look for him." Chris had taken off! My heart sank when I looked down the dark street and didn't see him. But then, I looked the other way and just caught him turning the corner. He was running on his toes wearing nothing but a diaper! Thank God, he turned left instead of right because right went toward the highway. He seemed to be going on a route that we'd taken before. He was very route-oriented so I said to myself, "Don't panic. He's going to follow the way we normally go." I sprinted down the block, leaped over a parked car, and found him. There he was, just sitting there very happy. "Hi, Chris." No reaction. He just smiled as I took him back to the house.

In a split second he had run out the door and down the street with no concern for anything! What if I hadn't found him? Surely the police would have questioned my competence as a parent, and I'm the most concerned parent in the world! I'm the one who always yells at everyone else to watch him more carefully. But what kind of parent could I be, the officer would wonder, with my son two blocks away in his diaper at night?

It was a rude awakening. I knew we had to do something fast to ensure Chris's safety. He wasn't even considered a significant runner, but we could not take the risk that he'd dash out of the house again. A lot of these kids take off any chance they get. You open the door – BANG! They're gone. They see a space. They're gone. It doesn't even matter if they're dressed or not. They just like to run. It is not unusual to find kids with autism miles away playing in front of restaurants or sitting in a gully unable to communicate. They have absolutely no concept of danger.

My wife, Jae, and I were talking about our hopes for Chris when the happy thought of his independence was quickly interrupted. "Wait a minute. What if he's out on his own and something happens? We have to introduce him to the police and get him fingerprinted right away!" But somehow that didn't seem like enough. What about all the other children with autism running off and not being able to explain who they are and where they live? What happens if a person with autism creates a public disturbance? How would a police officer deal with him? If emergency responders are not aware of autistic behaviors they won't recognize a child as having autism. Instead they will think he is mentally ill, on drugs, or just antagonistic. How would ambulance and hospital personnel know how to check and treat for injuries? How would a firefighter rescue a child with autism who is hidden away in the corner of a house unaware of danger?

The public tends either to be educated about disorders such as cerebral palsy and Down's syndrome or a disorder that is visible; not so with autism. This is the curse of the disorder. You have a normal- looking child with a host of socially unacceptable behaviors that no one understands. No two people with autism behave exactly alike, and people are always looking at you and your child

as if you're crazy. Often they give you dirty looks and act absolutely disgusted.

When we go to an amusement park we get a band that allows
us to go to the front of the line. It's absolutely necessary because
Chris can't stand on line for very long. But if I take him up front
and people have been standing on line for three hours in the sun, it
is not a pleasant scene. They see me cutting in line with this
normal-looking blond kid and want to kill me! I don't blame them.
But that's the curse of this disorder. And you can see how such a
typical situation lends itself to calling a cop or some other author-
ity to the scene.

The more I thought about safety issues, the clearer the solution
became. My local police precinct and other emergency workers
needed to be trained about autism, and I would be the one to do it.
Once I began the training I found that most emergency personnel
knew very little about autism unless they were previously exposed
to it. Typical comments were: "They're like the guy in the movie
Rain Man. What's his special skill? They're all smart, right?"

Dispelling these myths and stressing how difficult it is for
people with autism to communicate became a very important
focus of these training sessions. When emergency responders
don't know a person has autism or how to deal with it, the person
with the disability can get pushed around, put in jail, admit to
crimes they didn't commit, get injured, and even die. It's necessary
to understand the characteristics of autism and what an emergency
worker might encounter. It is important to learn how to make a
person with autism feel as safe, secure, and as unthreatened as
possible. So my training teaches not to get frustrated with
somebody who appears to be ignoring you. Don't get angry with
somebody who stands right up close to you, yells rather than
speaks, or talks robotically. Police learn not to attack somebody
who gets aggressive, spits, or bites.

Police, firefighters, emergency medical technicians and emergency room workers all know about alcoholics, diabetics, mental retardation, and cerebral palsy. They should also know about autism. Their mouths drop open at these training sessions when they learn about the disorder. They're saying to themselves, "This is shocking! I would have cuffed this guy. I would have knocked him out."

A general response at my training sessions is, "Thank God you told us about this because we didn't know about it and would have made serious mistakes. We had no idea this disorder was so severe and encompassed so many behaviors. Now if we encounter somebody with autism we'll know what to look for and have the confidence to handle the situation."

Police officers are trained in law enforcement to follow standard procedures for interactions with suspects. They are not often trained to identify the differences between unlawful behavior and behavior of the developmentally disabled. Not knowing how to interact with the disabled not only leads to dangerous outcomes, but also citizen complaints and lawsuits. So it's very important that emergency personnel receive this training. It gives them cues to look for, and reminds them that there are people in the community who don't fit their expectations. My son could be mistaken for a lot of things. I've seen the stares. But just because he's disabled doesn't mean he's stupid or a threat or should be locked away.

According to the 1999 National Victim Assistance Academy report funded by the US Department of Justice's Office for Victims of Crime, between four and five per cent of Americans have a developmental disability, including mental retardation, autism, cerebral palsy, and severe learning disabilities. The report states that individuals with disabilities are more likely than non-disabled individuals to be victims of crime including physical, sexual, and emotional abuse. In fact, they are reported to have a four to ten times higher risk of becoming crime victims than persons without a disability. The Academy says that crimes against these individuals are seriously underreported, and when reported, victims are not believed and cases are not prosecuted.

Disability training in the law enforcement field is also lacking. Some groups and agencies such as the Maryland Police and Correctional Training Commission have designed their own autism training programs for area law enforcement with great success. Other agencies such as the Texas Commission on Law Enforcement Officer Training and Education are using programs that encompass autism as well as other disabilities. But there is still a serious lack of education for emergency responders concerning autism and other disabilities. Organizations such as the Police Executive Research Forum (PERF) agree and are currently examining and developing disability training programs for law enforcement.

In the 3 August 1999 US Court of Appeals Tenth Circuit case, Gohier vs City of Colorado Springs (no. 98–1149), the judge also makes a case for better training. Referring to the Americans with Disabilities Act he says, "In order to comply with the non-discrimination mandate, it is often necessary to [train] public employees about disability. For example, persons who have epilepsy, and a variety of other disabilities, are frequently inappropriately arrested and jailed because police officers have not received proper training in [how to recognize and aid people having] seizures… Such discriminatory treatment based on disability can be avoided by proper training."

I assure you that these training sessions are not to teach complex therapy or to bash emergency workers by telling them they are politically incorrect and insensitive. My original autism training sessions were simply to identify my son to local workers so they would know him. They learned why they might be called to a scene, what behaviors they might see, and how to handle the situation. Now they and any other emergency personnel who receive training will know how to avoid negative encounters with people who have autism.

You're at the scene. The neighbor says this nut is biting himself, spinning and rocking, and peering into her window. His fingers are moving wildly, he's grunting and screaming. Would you know what to do?

Chapter 3

Characteristics of Autism

To handle encounters with autism effectively it is important for emergency responders to be informed about autism's behaviors. It is a disorder that can be very hard to detect, very strange, and very threatening. The person can appear typical-looking so you might immediately say to yourself, "He is a liar or a fake." I've had dozens of people say to me about my son, "He doesn't look bad at all. What's the big deal?" Or you might encounter kids with odd behaviors such as hair twirling, finger biting, finger play, teeth grinding, head rocking, or playing with spit. Different people have different habits. Autism is a complicated mishmash of hormones, intestinal ailments, genes, viruses, neurons, cells, enzymes and peptides. I know of one child who eats only tan foods. Another child can work on computer and add every number in existence, but is still in diapers because he's afraid of the toilet. It's a very strange disorder. The following is a list of many of the disorder's characteristics. A person with autism may have some, all, or varying degrees of each.

Self-stimulatory behavior

People with autism separate themselves from the rest of the world by not getting involved. I believe the mind and body are set up so you need stimulation, but when it's not gotten from your outside world, you do it for yourself with physical movements. Unfortunately, in order for people with autism to get stimulation they may behave in odd and self-injurious ways with their bodies. We call these self-stimulatory behaviors "stims."

Some persons with autism have very mild stims. Others have such drastic stims that they hurt themselves severely. Hand flapping, finger moving, head tapping, and head or body rocking are all common, repetitive behaviors (or stims) – none of which are harmful. Another stim is to fix on spinning or repetitive motions like falling snow, dropping grains of sand, falling leaves, or a spinning fan. All these behaviors seem to fill a void in an autistic person's solitary world of uninvolvement. But that may not be enough. So with the combination of being frustrated, not getting enough stimulation, and not fitting in they begin to hit themselves or self-inflict other pain.

Self-injurious behavior

The need to injure oneself probably comes after there has been no stimulation for a long time. These behaviors go far beyond repetitive behavior. There are severe cases of people who have simply knocked their heads into the wall, aimed for the sink and broken their heads open, or gouged their own eyes out. You will see these people wearing protective clothing and protective helmets. They're also on medication. It's sad, but they simply will hurt themselves at every chance they get if not stopped. Milder forms of self-stimulatory behaviors need not be stopped unless the person starts hurting him- or herself. It's just his or her way of venting or relaxing.

Can be violent

There may be times when people with autism have outbursts of violence. They do not intentionally try to hurt you, but unfortunately cannot control their behaviors. My son has bitten me so hard that he's taken skin off. Then he looks at me, rubs the wound, and hugs me as if he realizes what he has done and is sorry it has happened. Teenagers, in particular, have a greater tendency for violent outbursts due to huge hormonal imbalances. Remember, these kids already have hormone problems. Imagine what adolescence is like for them!

Insensitivity to pain

Do people with autism feel pain when they hurt themselves? Well, in most cases it seems that they have an insensitivity to pain. I've watched my son step with the bottoms of his feet on tacks and brambles and never flinch. In all probability because people with autism don't understand the concept of pain, don't want to deal with it, and are so adept at deferring things, they simply defer the pain and come back to it later. Then all of a sudden they realize they're hurt and get an overwhelming feeling of, "What happened?" It's not like when I put my hand on a tack and immediately respond, "Ow, ow, ow!" Two hours later they realize, "Wait a minute, my hand hurts," and then there's a lot of screaming because there's no conceptualization of what happened.

People with autism are so over-processed and so over-sensitive to things coming at them that they learn to defer pain and discomfort. Even when training to go to the bathroom, my son can defer that feeling of a full bladder. He's watching a movie, other noises are coming at him, and he doesn't concentrate on having to pee. So he goes in his pants and doesn't realize it. It's not till later that he'll look down and notice he's wet. It's the same thing with pain.

Aversion to touch

As a parent, you want to run over and console your child when he is hurt or upset, but usually there's not much you can do. Most people with autism have an aversion to hugs and cuddling. So whereas a typical child looks for his or her parents to kiss their "boo-boo" and give them a hug, a child with autism does not want to be touched at all. Touching can actually make things worse.

Avoidance of eye contact

Most people with autism don't like to be social and can appear to have a very stand-offish manner. It's not that they don't care particularly about communicating with you. It's just that they don't like to get involved in life. So you'll notice that autistics don't like to look at you. In fact, one of the first big things we do when working with them is say, "Look at me. Look at me." We're always trying to get that eye contact. Once you get eye contact there is more chance of achieving interactive communication.

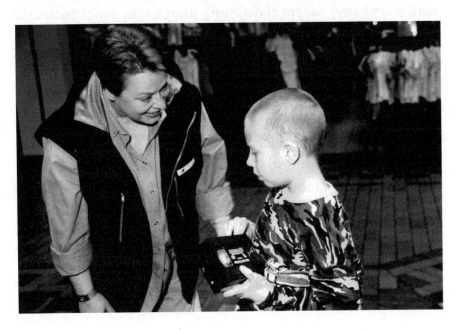

Unresponsive to normal teaching methods

Not only is it difficult to get children with autism to pay attention to you and interact, they are not responsive to normal teaching methods. They are visual learners who think in pictures. They also have uneven gross and fine motor skills.

Object spinning and preference for repetitive motion

Children with autism usually don't play with toys the way a typical child does. Because of their antisocial nature they don't mix with other children and have odd and uneven play skills. Although children with autism may appear aloof, most still want friends. Their disability, however, makes it extremely difficult to build those friendships. I'm sure if my son was able he'd tell you, "I'm a terribly intelligent and creative guy. I can't tell you a joke. I can't fit in. I don't have friends and I can't play like the other kids. It's frustrating. Being seven years old and unable to say I want to go to the movies, eat at McDonalds, or play like other kids feels awful."

A lot of these kids have a real fascination with spinning objects. I think it just takes them away from the world at hand. They're probably thinking, "I'm looking at this object. It's going to go around like this for twelve hours, and I'm very happy. I don't have to deal with anything that's going on around me. Everything else but this object is too much for me to deal with because I can't discern all that's happening." My son used to spin objects like disco balls for hours. Or he'd watch spinning fans and spinning lights. Just bang! He was off.

Extreme passivity or hyperactivity

In very young children, there is something called infantile autism in which the child is very passive. It's not uncommon when picking a baby up from his crib for him to go limp. I think that's their way of protecting themselves from getting involved with the world. They just don't want to deal with it. On the other hand, kids a little older with autism can engage in extreme activity where they won't stop running back and forth, often resembling caged animals.

Inappropriate laughter and crying

Kids with autism have been known to have inappropriate laughing and giggling spells that can last hours. My son laughs all the time and used to laugh in his sleep half the night. Despite what the experts say, I personally don't think it's inappropriate behavior. I merely think my son finds things funny that he's incapable of explaining. Just because he cracks up and doesn't say, "Dad, look at that movie. It's so funny," I don't think it's unacceptable laughter. I just think because society doesn't understand the humor it believes the behavior "looks" inappropriate.

Crying tantrums and extreme distress in reaction to what seems like nothing to a typical person are also characteristic of autism. I believe, however, that if we took the time to figure it out, we'd see that there was a very real reason for the crying. Perhaps we are unaware of something that is upsetting them. Or perhaps they're just reacting to physical discomfort they can't describe.

Nonverbal and non-responsive to verbal cues

A major block to communication is that many people with autism are nonverbal. They don't speak or have limited speech, and may sound expressionless or robotic. My son is considered basically nonverbal, but he and others like him do have means of communication. They may use a system of picture cards known as PECS, sign language, or a computer.

Persons with autism may also appear deaf because they are non-responsive to verbal cues. But in fact they usually test normal for hearing. Their non-responsiveness is most likely related to a need to isolate themselves from the surrounding world of sensory stimulation.

Echolalia

People with autism can be echolalic, repeating everything you say. So if you ask, "Do you need help?" they repeat, "Do you need help?"

"Do you need help?"

"Do you need help?"

They simply repeat everything you say. Why? It's probably because they don't know what you want from them and don't really understand the purpose of language. Remember, also, they don't like to participate in the world around them. So you're trying to engage in conversation with someone who doesn't want or know how to converse with you. Adult autistics have told me, "I repeated everything the guy said because I thought that's maybe what he wanted. When someone would ask, 'How are you today?' I'd answer, 'How are you today?' In my head I was thinking, okay, now leave me alone."

So a person with echolalia is probably repeating your words hoping you'll go away. "Maybe if I just say what he says, he will shut up." They don't mean to be disrespectful or belligerent.

Inappropriate attachment

Another characteristic of autism is "inappropriate" attachment to objects; a word I don't like. I think it's more a balance issue. They have a lot of vestibular problems and may carry objects for balance. For instance, when teaching motor skills, it's much easier to teach the child to pick up a cup to his mouth than directing him to do something like cross his hands with outstretched arms. Apparently the cup acts as an anchor to balance them. Another theory is that the object brings a little order to their world. "As long as I have this in my hand, everything is fine." It's like a security blanket. And like a security blanket, they must have it with them at all times.

The objects they pick can be anything. My son used to carry around laminated logos wherever he went. One time he dropped a logo behind a store shelf and started screaming. It was a major tantrum. I didn't even know what was wrong until I saw he didn't have the logo in his hand. Thank goodness I found it after digging around! Once he had it again he was fine, but he just needed to have that logo in his hand. Now what normal person would find a screaming toddler and think he lost his logo? Without under-standing behaviors of autism, it's impossible to understand how to communicate effectively with a person who has the disorder.

Order and routine

People with autism don't like their routines changed. So you can see a kid absolutely out of sorts, throwing a complete tantrum because a TV show at nine o'clock didn't run. He had to see that show on this TV at this time. And there's nothing you can do about it. You can't explain it to them. Every morning Chris and I walk and get donuts. Well, if we don't go it sets off a fit. I've seen dozens of kids who had absolute fits and seizures because their routine was changed.

These kids look to bring order to a world that's out of order to them. There's noise and lights and things coming at them all the time. "So how do I stop things from coming at me? How do I make this world orderly for myself? Well, I establish a routine. I line things up because it makes my life orderly for me, and that makes me happy. I flick the switch on and off because when I flick it on the light comes on. When I flick it off the light goes off. It makes everything ordered. I know what's going to happen."

Use others as a tool to get what they want

A lot of kids with autism will indicate need by moving you to get what they want. They're very afraid of becoming actively involved in life. They won't get anything themselves, even if it's something they desire. So a child with autism might take you by the hand, bring you over, and put your hand on a soda bottle because he wants a soda. When Chris started showing signs of autism you could have walked in my house as a total stranger, and he would never look up or be bothered. But if he wanted to eat, for instance, he would take you by the hand and put it on the refrigerator door. Then he'd put your hand in the refrigerator once you opened the door and put it on the food he wanted. Pointing is not a usual behavior for someone with autism. In some way it forces them to be more of an active participant in life. So learning to point is a big step forward.

Oblivious to emotions

One guy with autism told me he didn't know what his mother looked like for the first ten years of his life because he didn't have any reason to look at her. He didn't want to look at her, didn't need her, and didn't want her in his life. "Leave me alone," was his attitude. Very detached. Naturally, a person like this would have little instinct about others' emotions and facial gestures. They've never learned to key in on these. (Temple Grandin, a famous author with autism, had to be taught what jealousy was. Somebody was jealous of her, and she didn't understand what that meant: a brilliant woman who's a PhD.)

Another good example of emotional detachment is a research study that used typical toddlers and toddlers with high functioning autism. The children were told, "Put these pictures of men into groups any way you like." Three men were smiling, three men were sad, and three were angry. The normally developing toddlers grouped the pictures according to emotion. The kids with autism grouped the pictures according to what hats the men were wearing: a perfect example of not paying attention to emotion. It means nothing to them. The first thing a typical person keys in on is the smiling face. That's what hits you first. But the person with autism thinks, "Oh, look at that hat."

Fear of animals

Obsessive fear of animals is another characteristic of autism. My son is deathly afraid of dogs. I've seen him fall down and just collapse when a dog comes by. He's getting better around them, but his reaction is still very unpredictable. We try very hard to steer clear of dogs and explain our dilemma to neighbors who are dog owners.

Inappropriate response to noise

Another typical behavior of autism is an inappropriate response to noise. A phone ringing can absolutely overwhelm some kids with autism so that they begin screaming. Others can be so good at filtering everything out that they don't pay any attention to noise. I can drop dishes behind my son and he won't turn around. This is so dangerous. Think how treacherous it is to navigate the world if you don't hear traffic noises or someone yelling "stop" or "be careful!"

No fear of danger

Now compound an inappropriate response to noise with another characteristic of autism: no fear of danger. People with autism will run into traffic and not realize there's danger. They cue out the traffic activity and cross the street with oncoming cars and trucks! Every time I take my son across the street I say, "Chris, cars." Of course I still have to hold his hand because he might not hear me and walk in the street anyway.

Danger just doesn't occur to them. That's why you see kids disappear. They'll walk out of the mall or walk out of their family's home because they want to go to a place of comfort or get away from what's bothering them. They don't think they're doing anything wrong. They just don't know. Kids have been known to disappear in the woods, go to a quiet place, and lie there for days because they're comfortable. They don't realize they're supposed to tell their mothers where they are, or that somebody misses them. All that conceptualization is gone. It just doesn't occur to them. Consequences of behavior don't mean anything to them so fear is not something they understand.

CHARACTERISTICS OF AUTISM – AN OVERVIEW

Self-stimulatory behavior

- ○ Hand flapping
- ○ Finger moving/play
- ○ Head tapping
- ○ Head or body rocking
- ○ Spinning self
- ○ Watching spinning objects, i.e., ceiling fans, tops
- ○ Transfixing on objects: snowflakes, falling leaves, grains of sand.

Self-stimulatory behavior need not be stopped or interfered with.

Self-injurious behavior

- ○ Head butting
- ○ Head banging
- ○ Self-biting
- ○ Eye gouging
- ○ Scratching

Self-injurious behavior **needs** to be stopped.

Aggressive behavior

- ○ Head butting
- ○ Biting
- ○ Punching

Aggressive behavior can be caused by over-stimulation, fear, pain, surprise, or a lack of communication. Although you may have to protect yourself, you do not have to be overly aggressive. Remember – this person does not mean to hurt you. Try to restrain with quiet control. If person is restrained, check his physical condition frequently for choking, vomiting, or severe discomfort.

Insensitivity to pain
People with autism are not always aware of pain or able to communicate pain or injury. Major physical trauma may go unnoticed. However, minor scrapes and cuts may be perceived as major. Check thoroughly for injuries, especially at the scene of an accident or crime.

Aversion to touch
Being touched can be perceived as pain. Don't touch the neck, face, or approach from behind. People with autism don't like surprises.

Avoidance of eye contact
Most people with autism will not look directly at you. Some will look at you with a peripheral glance, through spread fingers, through spread tree branches. Don't mistake avoidance of eye contact as guilt or belligerence.

Lack of response to normal teaching methods
People with autism respond to visual cues. Many police departments now carry sets of visual communication cards.

Spinning objects – preference for repetitive motion
- May be constantly spinning a ball in his/her hand or rapidly switching a ball from hand to hand
- May stare at flashing lights, ceiling fans, etc.

○ May appear trance-like.

Don't mistake for drug use, mental illness, or lack of respect.

Extreme passivity or hyperactivity

○ May go limp at touch

○ May appear listless

○ May want to run or bolt

○ May rapidly pace back and forth

○ If verbal, may flip from idea to idea or speak rapidly

○ May want to leave scene immediately and seek comfort zone.

Inappropriate laughter and crying

○ May laugh and cry for hours for no apparent reason

○ May show extreme distress over minor incidents.

Echolalic and echoic behavior

○ May repeat exactly what you say

○ Voice may sound monotonous or robotic

○ May mimic your voice.

Don't mistake for belligerence.

Nonverbal and non-responsive to verbal cues

○ Limited or no speech

○ May appear deaf

○ May communicate with sign language, pointing, picture cards, computer devices.

Don't mistake non-responsiveness for guilt or lack of interest.

"Inappropriate" attachment

- ○ May be holding unusual or seemingly unimportant items that are critically important to the child.
- ○ Items may include toys, rocks, acorns, cards, torn page, shapes, fabric, etc.

Do not take away or child may become extremely agitated!

Need for order and routine

- ○ Obsessive need for timeliness and routine
- ○ May repeatedly ask to be taken to a certain place or see a certain show at a specific time.

Trivial as these requests may seem, they are extremely important to a person with autism.

Use of others as tool to get what they want

- ○ Will take you by hand to get what they need – drink, tissue, opening door.

Simple acts can cause great trepidation.

Obliviousness to emotions

- ○ May not understand facial expressions, i.e., smiling
- ○ May not understand jokes
- ○ May not understand they are the victim of a crime
- ○ May be hard to diffuse situation with normal socialization techniques.

Inappropriate response to noise

- ○ May cover ears with hands
- ○ May try to break object causing discomfort

○ May appear deaf

○ May not respond to verbal command.

Fear of animals

○ May have obsessive fear of animals, especially dogs

○ May fear unexpected behavior of the animal

○ May hate loud barking.

Remove animals or take person to quiet setting.

No fear of danger

○ May run into traffic

○ May bolt suddenly into street

○ May willingly go with strangers

○ May not recognize dangerous situations

○ May not have understanding of fire, heat, sharp objects.

Chapter 4

Why Law Enforcement might be Called

For law enforcement officers especially, why would you be called to the scene because of a person who has autism? What would you find there? Often you are called into unexpected situations, not knowing what you're going to find. That's why it's especially important to be prepared for a surprise encounter with a person who has autism.

Self-stimulatory and self-injurious behavior

When people don't know how to deal with situations or know what to do, they tend to go to the authorities. Self-injurious behavior, self-stimulatory behavior, and repetitive behavior are actions that may cause such calls to the police. If a citizen saw someone in the street flapping his hands or hitting himself, that might be considered very strange behavior and reason to call law enforcement. Certainly if someone was seen banging her head against the wall, police would be called right away. Once at the scene, there really is no reason for law enforcement officers to stop any stimulatory behaviors unless the person is hurting him or herself. The best resolution would be to call the person's parents or caretakers to come and take her home.

Wandering alone

Somebody in the neighborhood may call you because they see a child wandering alone. A lot of kids with autism are runners. That means the minute the door or window is open, they're gone. Bang! They just run. The child may be undressed even if it's cold or rainy. He may be walking down the middle of a busy street or sitting in the woods. He may be running into oncoming traffic, walking into a neighbor's home, or climbing into a car.

Please remember, the parents of these children are not irre-sponsible! Sure, you find a kid naked three miles away, he's crossed two highways, and you want to confront the mother asking, "What kind of mother are you?" But this is just one of the many difficult challenges of autism. My son is not typically a runner, although he, too, has walked out of the door in his diaper and left. There have been times when he's gone out the back door and just disappeared into the bushes.

Peering into windows

Peering into windows is another big police call because many autistics have a propensity to look into windows. They appear to be peeping Toms, but in reality their motives are quite innocent. I believe people with autism are actually attracted to windows because of the framing. If you think about it, the framing makes everything around it unimportant. So if you go to a house and look into the window it's like looking at a TV. By focusing just on that window, you're able to see a scene. You might see a person sitting on the sofa reading, but it has nothing to do with you. It's removed. You don't have to touch them, and they don't have to talk to you because you're outside their world. That's a very comforting feeling to someone with autism. When we'd take walks my son would love to put his head against a window and look inside. I'd tell him, "Come on, Chris. Somebody lives there. You can't do that." But peering into windows is very pleasurable for them. Unfortunately, they are invading the privacy of others and look like peeping Toms.

Turning on water faucets

Remember how repetitive actions like turning lights on and off are comforting to autistics? In the same manner many kids with autism have been found at strangers' houses turning water spigots on and off, on and off.

Suspected drug abuse or mental illness

Many behaviors of autism can resemble mental illness or drug abuse in an older child. The person may seem absolutely crazy or potentially violent. In these circumstances law enforcement is bound to be called. Imagine you see somebody standing outside your home peering into your window, flapping his hands, and biting himself. You're going to call the police.

A kid with autism doesn't have the social awareness to know that tapping his head looks bad, crazy, or funny. My son will stand in the middle of a room when he's excited and yell and flap his hands. I think it's sweet because that's his way of being excited. But if someone saw him in the street, especially if he was a teenager, they'd call the police. After all, here's a big guy flapping his hands and screaming. Anyone would think that's odd behavior.

Bizarre or disruptive behavior

Not understanding social cues is another major reason for misinterpretation of behavior that leads to police calls. Once a huge bodybuilder who lives in my complex was sitting in a lounge chair that my son, Chris, liked. So Chris went over, reached down, and grabbed the bodybuilder by the crotch to get him out of the chair. The guy naturally started yelling for him to stop. I smoothed things over with an explanation, but you can imagine how different this scene would have played if I hadn't been there. As a law enforcement officer called to a scene, expect similar behavior. You may say, "Step back, please." And the kid may continue to come right up to your face.

Here's another example of a social miscue leading to trouble. I know of a boy who likes to tickle under arms and around breasts. His mother tries to control him with behavioral management, but he still went up to a strange woman in the mall and tickled her breasts. You can imagine the woman's reaction! Of course the boy's actions were misinterpreted.

Toe walking is another peculiar behavior that attracts attention. Staring into space and slowly walking on toes can make people with autism look very unbalanced, almost as if in a drug-induced state. Robotic speech and robotic movements are other peculiar behaviors that tend to attract negative attention from the public.

Involvement in altercations

I was watching my son on our monitor when his shirt got hung up on the post of the chair and he couldn't move. He just stood there. Saddest thing I ever saw. So I went up to him and said, "Chris, say 'help me' or pick up your shirt." He would have just stayed there. He didn't scream or anything. His attitude was "this is the situation

I'm in and I don't know that I'm supposed to ask for help or get out of this." So there he stood. Very sad.

A young man with autism was in a store and took a candy bar. The clerk yelled at him and the man put it back, but then the clerk started shoving him. Why didn't the young man call the police? Why didn't he ask for help if he was trapped in the store? It's because autistics don't know to ask for help. So you may very well find yourself called to a scene where someone with autism is mixed up in a fight, and doesn't know he needs assistance.

Hitting or biting other children

Last night my son, Chris, was outside with his sister playing with a bunch of kids who were throwing grass and rolling around. Suddenly he stopped, his lip tightened, and he started angrily going toward a kid. Luckily, I was watching him and went over. "Chrissie, come to Daddy." Why he became angry I don't know. Maybe he was over-stimulated, maybe he was overcrowded, maybe they were pushing him a bit, or maybe there were too many faces near him. But if I didn't call him over and snap him out of it, he might have bitten, smacked, or grabbed that boy. And what might the father of that child have done? Called the police, pressed charges, or screamed.

We try to teach Chris to control his behavior, but sometimes he becomes so overwhelmed from stimulation that he loses all ability for self-control. Is his behavior acceptable? No. Is it his fault? No. Does he deserve to be screamed at or thrown in jail? No. But most people do not understand the effects of autism and assume the person is just a bully. If knowledgeable police officers are called, however, they can help defuse the situation before it escalates into something further.

Suspected child abuse

Picture this scene. You're in a restaurant and you see a kid bite his parent. When the parent restrains the child, the child starts hitting himself and the parent restrains him even more. Then the child bites the parent again. As a customer or restaurant manager you might be thinking to yourself, "Something's wrong. This child is hitting himself, and this situation is out of control. Perhaps there's a possible case of abuse here and somebody should step in. Would I be remiss if I ignore this?" You can see where genuine concern might lead to a call to the police. But as a law enforcement officer, it is imperative that you thoroughly investigate the circumstances. If you find that the child has a disability like autism, then your initial reaction should be that child abuse is probably not a factor here.

> When I took over police training the guys here didn't even know what autism was. Then Bill Davis called and offered some training to educate us about the disorder. The man's phenomenal. Before his training we didn't know what we were looking for when there were encounters with autism. The men approached the persons as if they were on drugs. And anyone on drugs is absolutely getting cuffed, taken to the hospital, and getting a complete drug screen with a urinalysis and blood drawn. But of course the person is not on drugs; he has autism and the situation is only going to escalate.
>
> I highly recommend the training. The most important thing we learned was to look for the signs that would tell us this is autism. The officers now know to keep the subject calm, talk to him, and soothe him rather than reach out and grab him and try and handcuff and restrain him. They now also know to get in contact with someone who understands the disorder who can help out if necessary. The training was so beneficial that I'm bringing Bill Davis back because I've had a bunch of new officers start and also I want to refresh

the older guys. (Sergeant David P. Odenwalt, Sr., Lancaster Bureau of Police)

WHY LAW ENFORCEMENT MIGHT BE CALLED – AN OVERVIEW

Self-stimulatory and self-injurious behavior

- Repetitive actions
- Hand flapping
- Finger play
- Rocking, spinning
- Head banging
- Self-biting
- Pinching or scratching self
- Punching self
- Thrashing.

Wandering alone

- Child appears to be unaccompanied by an adult and unconcerned with his situation
- May dart into traffic
- May be dressed inappropriately for the weather, and be seemingly unconcerned.

Children with autism are often attracted to water and may wander into ponds, lakes, and pools. Check these areas carefully if a child is reported missing.

- **Peering into windows**
- **Turning water faucets on and off**

- **Behavior may mimic drug abuse or mental illness**
- **Bizarre or disruptive behavior**
    - Lining up objects: twigs, stones, CDs, cassettes, etc.
    - Pica: eating inappropriate objects such as rocks, mud, glass
    - Toe walking
    - Robotic-like speech

Involvement in altercations

- May commit a crime without understanding that they did something wrong.

Hitting or biting other children

Suspected child abuse

- Parent may be restraining child with what may appear to be questionable force in response to the child's escalating, violent behavior.
- Parent may be wrapping arms around child from behind.

Chapter 5

How to Communicate

Now that you can identify some behaviors of autism, how do you approach a person with autism in an emergency? Most often you'll come to an incident not knowing the person has autism and approach things as you normally do. I hope there will be enough cues for you to start to notice this is not a typical child or adult. As you observe, you'll see there is some developmental delay or neurological problem preventing a typical response.

Look for ID

If you've evaluated the situation and determined that the person has a disability, your first step is easy. Immediately look for an ID tag or bracelet that will give you some information. We use a tag on the shoe that simply states "Christopher Davis, nonverbal autistic," and his phone number. It is very noticeable on his shoe and is the only place he'll allow it. In fact, Chris can't stand having anything on his body. If there's a tag on his neck, wrist, or shirt he'll take it off. He once sat in the back seat of the car wearing a sweater with raised numbers on it, and he chewed them off. Be aware also that families are now using decals on car and house windows. These decals will alert you to the fact that there is a person with autism inside.

Immediately call contact person

If you find an ID, call the parents or contact immediately! They will usually know how you can calm the person down until they can get there.

Ask contact person to register child with police

Once the parent or contact person does arrive, mention to them that it's very important to register with the police. Tell them to give a photo, phone number, address, and the child's major characteristics of the disorder. Does he or she run away or bite? If someone with autism is registered you can immediately find out who he is and react accordingly. It is a necessary step that will make your job a lot easier.

Prepare for a long encounter

Let's say you can't find a contact person or information about the person who you suspect has autism. He or she is probably not going to respond right away, so prepare yourself for a long encounter – unless, of course, this is an emergency situation when you don't have time.

Remain calm

Remember, calmness is important. Use calm body language – no gesticulating, no waving or pointing, no rapid stuff, and no screaming and yelling. Let's say you command, "Come to the car," but the person doesn't comply. So you say louder and more insistently, "Come to the car!" That's not going to matter. The volume or the sternness aren't going to matter. These things don't register.

If you read him his rights it doesn't mean he understands just because you repeat them or say them loudly. And it also doesn't mean he understood them because he said "yes".

Keep commotion down

When you are dealing with persons who have autism be aware that they have very protective responses to over-stimulation. That's why you want to keep commotion down to a minimum. Get them away from loud sounds and bright lights, for example. Sound and light are harsh and upsetting to them. Remove odors. My son gags at odors. I once ate a liverwurst sandwich and he ran to the corner and threw up. The smell just overwhelmed him. Once we all ordered broccoli in a diner and when it was placed on the table Chris started gagging and falling over from the smell. We had it taken away and he was fine as soon as it was removed. Smells hit him very hard. So you have to understand that. He's not like you.

Keep animals away

Canine cops, take note! People with autism can have an obsessive fear of animals. My son's eyes roll in his head, he collapses, and starts biting himself if a dog is near. An uninformed reaction would be, "Calm down. What's the matter with you?" But the appropriate reaction would be to remove the dog. If you're a canine cop and you know you're responding to a call with a person who has autism, please keep your dog in the car! Otherwise call another officer to handle the situation.

Repeat short, direct phrases

Use short direct phrases and repeat them over and over again. If I said to my son, "Come down the stairs. Get your jacket. Come on. We're going to go to dinner," he'd probably only hear dinner. Instead I say, "Come on. Let's eat. Let's eat." If I repeat it enough he's going to hear that last word and know he's going to eat. You want to look at your subject and say, "Come here. Come here. Come here," repeating it until you get the eye contact.

It's very important to try to get the individual to focus on you with his or her eyes. Normally, when a person looks and pays attention their eyebrows go up. But for people who have autism the muscles that lift the eyebrows are often underdeveloped. It is not easy to get them to pay attention. So always start by saying, "Look at me. Look at me," and direct that eye contact. Keep your phrases short and direct the gaze with your hand by bringing it first toward their eyes and then toward yours.

Non-response does not imply guilt

Don't interpret non-response as a negative. Normally, if someone seemed not to care about what you were saying and was not looking at you, how would you interpret that? He's deceitful. But in this case not making eye contact or answering you has absolutely nothing to do with guilt.

Body language, facial expressions, social cues and jokes usually don't work with autistic individuals. They don't get it. You can smile at a typical little child and say, "Hi. I'm here to help. Here's a lollipop," and it works. But all the things you know work with a typical child aren't going to get a response from a child with autism. So you have to pause and think, "This is not the typical person I'm working with."

Don't touch or take by the hand

You should not take the individual by the hand and lead him, either. In a normal situation you would take a child's hand and lead him away. In this situation that is not something you should do. Don't touch or push unless it's a complete emergency. If you're in a fire and able to get to this person but unable to coax him, you're obviously going to have to grab him. If he's injured you'll have to put him on a gurney. But otherwise if you take him by the hand he might be absolutely petrified and act violently to you or himself. You also want to stay away from the neck; don't touch people with autism near the face, and don't approach them from behind. A touch in the wrong place could cause the child to go limp or absolutely berserk.

Ironically, there could also be a situation where a stranger takes the hand of a child with autism and the child goes. Or a stranger says, "Come with me," and the child goes. You just don't know how they'll react.

Use soft gestures

You must use very soft gestures to get the child's attention rather than touching or grabbing a hand. In other words, you're waiting for a comfortable feeling of eye contact. I always say to Chris, "Look at me. Look at me." When he looks, then I'll softly tell him what to do. You may have to repeat yourself twenty times before you can reach that point.

Use direct language and avoid idioms

Avoid idiomatic expressions. There's a story about a child with autism who went to kindergarten and the teacher told him his job was to keep his eye on the coats. So the child went over and stared at the coats and wouldn't move because that's what he had been told to do. If you tell a kid to "spread eagle", the kid won't know what you're talking about. Idioms are absolutely foreign, so use direct language. If you want the person to come to the car, you would have to say, "Come to the car," or "Come car." Very plain and very direct.

Don't interpret odd behaviors as belligerent

Because people with autism may defer everything you say or want to get you out of their face, they may not look at you or respond to your commands. They might even cover their ears – a lot of kids with autism do this. Often you'll see them cover their ears or shake their heads back and forth when the phone rings just to get past the noise. So if it's a tense situation and the person is flapping, he'll probably turn away when you come up and say, "Hey, come here a minute." That doesn't mean he's being a wise guy or belligerent; it doesn't mean he's escaping, lying, or he's guilty. He's just reacting to the way his autism is controlling him.

The person you're going to encounter may be echolalic, which means he will repeat what you say to him. Picture this. The police officer says, "Hi, buddy. What's the matter?" The boy, who's echolalic, answers, "Hi, buddy. What's the matter?" "What, are you a wise guy? Why are you repeating what I say to you?" You have to understand this is a neurological affliction, not belligerence.

Usually kids do things to comfort themselves. My son will sing the ABC song when he's stressed. You may get a kid who's a little verbal who goes to a topic he finds soothing. He knows that information is information. It rings true all the time and brings order to his world. Let's say he knows the US presidents in order – so what happens when he is confronted with questions? "The first president of the United States is George Washington, the second president of…"

The police officer then asks, "What are you telling me that for?" Because it makes him feel better. He's going back to something that he knows. He can't ad lib and doesn't want to deal with what you're talking about. So he goes back to something that's comforting. He might name every state capital or race car driver because that's what he knows and gives him comfort.

Understand different forms of communication

The person you're going to encounter may be nonverbal. That's a big communication block, obviously. This is not a person who's going to say, "I'm upset." But he or she may have other means of communication. It's very important to know some of the different ways in which people with autism can communicate. There are now high tech devices called Dyna Voxes and Dyna Mites. These are little computers that are programmed to suit the individual. Communication is achieved by pressing different category buttons. One category might be "emergency situations." So the help button is pressed and says, "Help me" in a computer voice.

If asked, "Where do you live, son?" my child could press the button that says "My name is Chris. I live at 140 Elm." The voice can be programmed for a child's voice, an adult's voice, a male or female voice, and the program can be as complicated or as simple as you want. Some of the computers are made very small so you can just carry them around for emergency situations such as fire, bathroom, pain, and hospital. When pressed they say, "Please help me, call the police, or call my parents."

Another communication device is a signboard. It's set up like a keyboard, but you have to see which letter is depressed as it's typed and then spell it out yourself. It also has keys for the words yes and no. Usually the person's hand is held lightly to help control their stims. So if you've got the person's attention, quietly ask, "Are you hurt?" He can type out "yes" or "no" with a signboard or maybe type the word "head" if it hurts.

Chris communicates with PECS, Picture Exchange Communication System. It's a series of universal communication icons with Velcro that a child uses to form sentences on a board or book. The whole idea is to take the frustration out of communicating. The theory behind PECS is to enhance language and ensure interactive communication. For instance, if a child points without first getting a person's attention, the attempt to communicate may fail. But when using pictures in a hand-to-hand exchange, communication failures are usually prevented. In addition, the pictures are more easily understood than pointing or signing. They can be large or small enough to fit in a wallet.

I have a small board that fits in Chris's pocket and hooks on his belt. Therefore he always has a means of communication. Let's say you ask him, "What's your mom's name?" He'll flip through his book and find a photo of his mom that says "My mom is Jae." You can ask him questions or he can actually talk to you on his own. There's a universal symbol with hands outstretched for the words

"I want." He might put that on the Velcro strip, for instance, and place a picture of a soda can with the word soda next to it. Then he'll hand it to you.

He just made a sentence! Don't ignore him. "Oh, you want a soda? Okay, we'll get you a soda." Affirm that you understand him and give him the immediate reward. Some people make the mistake of saying, "Very good, you're communicating with us." But then they don't follow through with getting him what he requests. Remember to give the person what they communicated for as an immediate reward if you can. This will help the communication and the understanding.

Use picture cards to aid communication

One other communication aid you might want to use is picture cards. There are people and businesses now that distribute picture cards for just these very circumstances. They help victims identify suspects, show what happened, and whether they need something. They're a simple, inexpensive way to turn a frustrating experience into a smooth-going one.

Perhaps you can get your hospital or fire department to keep a set. That way both you and the child can communicate easily. In fact, no matter what area of emergency response you're in, it's advisable to keep picture cards on hand. They will be invaluable for communicating with people who have a variety of disabilities.

Don't expect a lot of information or tactfulness

Even if they are verbal or have some form of communication, the autistic person may still not be able to give the information you want. "Somebody took your wallet. What did he look like?" Well, the person with autism probably never looked at the thief. They don't look at people. "What do you mean you didn't look at him?

The guy robbed you! Where were you?" "I don't know." Don't expect a whole lot of information.

People with autism also have very weak self-help skills so if they don't understand what you're saying, they're not going to ask for clarification. You're not going to hear, "I don't quite understand what you want from me," or "I wasn't doing anything wrong," or "This guy attacked me." They may not think that the attack was severe or they may have already dealt with it in their own minds.

Some people with autism may repeat one word like "no" all the time. "Can you come here and tell me…"

"No."

"I want to talk to you."

"No."

People with autism can also be bluntly honest without tact. In a way that's good because they don't lie. I don't believe they have the ability to lie. It's got to be taught to them. So you might be called to a kid who has autism, and while talking to him he might say, "By the way, you are ugly," or "You are fat," or "You are rude." They are brutally honest, loving, sensitive people, but they appear to be wise guys. Try to help them along.

Don't get angry at anti-social behaviors

Volume may also be off if the person speaks. My son can be very loud and we have to give him the sign to bring his volume down. You may say to a kid, "Are you okay?" And he may scream, "I'M FINE!!" A real scream! They just don't know that they're loud because they miss all social cues.

They may also sound oddly robotic. When my son, Chris, wants to get out of the bathtub he says in a robotic voice, "Get out pull plug." A lot of these kids have monotone or computer-like voices. We were swimming and Chris said the same thing, "Get out pull plug." To him that whole phrase means I want to get out of the water. I understood what he wanted, and to me it wasn't strange. But you can imagine what somebody hearing that might think: here's a normal-looking, big, blond healthy boy swimming with his dad and he's talking like a robot.

There are a number of other socially unacceptable behaviors as well. Some autistic people spit or play with their spit. They may go up and touch you in the face, touch your private parts, stare right at you, or go right up to your face and stick their nose in it. To them they're not doing anything wrong. It's not that they aren't taught not to do this stuff. It just has no significance for them. As a person with autism I may not be able to recognize things from your point of view because I can't think that way. I can't conceptualize like that. We know as social beings that if you pinch a policeman he is going to get angry. These kids just may come up and do that, but they can't predict that reaction.

Unless you want things to escalate you're going to have to recognize that there's a disorder going on here! You have to lose your whole typical mode of thinking. So if you come upon a kid who's not talking, is flapping his hand, and then comes up and tickles you in your private parts, you have to say to yourself, "That's not normal. I have to back off." Realize these actions are not meant to antagonize, and calmly repeat, "Don't do that." It is to be hoped that the behavior will eventually stop, but if it doesn't that's okay. The most important point is not to get angry!

Common responses to expect

People with autism find it very hard sometimes to respond and will try to guess at what you're asking. They feel pressured to give you an answer so they get very anxious. If you've ever experienced anxiety you know how your body can lose control. Suddenly you're sweating, your foot's tapping uncontrollably, and you're stammering. Now you have to fight to control all these things. Think how hard it is for you, then think how hard it is for someone with autism to control her anxiety when all her hormones and neurons are out of sync.

A typical kid responds to your questions. A kid with autism probably won't answer or will give you unusual responses to simple questions. It doesn't means he's hiding something or plotting. Ask a typical suspect, "Did you take that briefcase?" His answer might be, "Bob told me to, but I didn't know what was in it." The person with autism might answer, "Yes. Yes." You then ask why and he again answers, "Yes. Yes." Listen. The real thief is talking to you, but the person with autism is giving the same answer over and over again. You can see there is a communication problem. If he's verbal he'll probably respond with a one-word answer, go to a topic that's comforting, or repeat what you say. For instance:

Cop: "Did you deliver that package?"

Child: "Did you deliver that package?"

Cop: "I said did you deliver that package?"

Child: "Did you deliver that package?"

Cop: "Don't be a wise guy with me."

Child: "Don't be a wise guy."

Obviously something's wrong here. Here's what happens if the person with autism goes to a subject that's comforting:

Cop: "Did you deliver that package?"

Child: "I like Muppets."

Cop: "What, are you crazy? I said, did you deliver that package?"

Child: "I like Muppets. The Muppets are Fozzie, Piggy…"

Or she might list the state capitals. What criminal would say, "Here are the capitals of the United States?" A person with autism might also repeat, "Yesterday I watched a program at 12:30. It was on Channel 7. It's on 12:30 on Thursday, March 11." That's a lot different from "I was with my boyfriend yesterday."

Let's say you got my son to the station house and you put him in a quiet room and you calmed him down; you'd see a great change from his behavior at the initial scene. Now if you put a guy who just robbed a store in a quiet room and said to him, "I want to ask you about this store," he still might say, "I told you I didn't know anything about the store!" My son's attitude would change far more than the criminal or drug user's attitude. If a drug user is high, he's high. He's going to be high in the quiet room too.

If you weren't sure my son had autism and asked him, "Hey, little guy, can I get you a candy bar?" he probably wouldn't know to answer you. A typical little guy would probably respond, "Can I have a soda, please?" Another child, with autism, might answer, "Trains, trains. The first train in the United States was 1899. The first train in the United States was 1899."

A light should go off in your head at this point. "This is not a criminal. This is not somebody I should come down on." Law enforcement officers have to calm themselves suddenly and behave very differently with suspects who have autism. They now have to coax a suspect quietly to relax. That is not easy after being trained to respond aggressively to attacks and antagonistic situations.

HOW TO COMMUNICATE – AN OVERVIEW

What you may encounter at the scene

- Child may be nonverbal
- Child may be echolalic or echoic
- When approached, child may run away
- May exhibit "fight or flight" behaviors
- May cover ears when being questioned
- May look away constantly
- May begin self-stimulatory behaviors when excited or nervous
- May not be able to ask for clarification of questions or situation
- May appear argumentative or belligerent
- May respond "no," "yes," or "why" to all questions
- May not understand body language, social cues, jokes, teasing
- May appear not to hear or care about what you are saying
- May avoid eye contact
- May have monotone voice
- May exhibit bad articulation
- May be poor judge of volume
- May play with spit
- May spit
- May have sensitivity to light, sound, smell, textures, temperatures
- May exhibit eating disorders

- ○ May be poor judge of personal space – may stand too close
- ○ May touch private parts
- ○ During stressful questioning, may obsessively speak of topic that comforts them or have extreme knowledge of, e.g., state capitals
- ○ May not be able to predict reactions from people or see things from a different point of view
- ○ May have difficulty distinguishing between minor and serious problems
- ○ May have weak self-help skills
- ○ May be bluntly honest.

Communication tips

- ○ Look for personal ID
- ○ Immediately call contact person (precinct should have telephone number of the local chapter of the National Autism Society or support group if no contact person is available)
- ○ Use direct, short phrases
- ○ Allow for delayed responses
- ○ Avoid idiomatic language
- ○ Repeat requests calmly and softly
- ○ Avoid rapid movement and pointing
- ○ Keep hands down
- ○ Wait for eye contact (*lack of eye contact does not mean guilt or deceit*)
- ○ Do not touch neck or face

- Do not approach from behind
- Don't stand too close
- Do not stop repetitive behaviors unless self-injurious
- Be aware of seizure disorders
- Evaluate very carefully for injury
- Be aware of protective responses to odors, light, sound, touch, temperatures, and animals
- Be aware of alternative means of communication, e.g., computers, yes/no signboards, picture exchange cards
- If arrested or restrained, put in quiet, safe surroundings away from others.

Remember that subject may not understand his rights even though he agrees.

Remember, people with autism may only process last word or two of what's said.

Chapter 6

Challenging Circumstances
for Emergency Responders

A father once told me a story about his daughter with autism who was at the mall with a new therapist. It turned out the girl hadn't been given the right medications and, while in the bathroom, she immediately went to the sink and banged her head hard enough to crack it open! The therapist was totally distraught, and the police were called. Now the police had to be convinced the woman really was the therapist, and the girl really had a disorder that caused this behavior. The officers, uninformed about autism, had a hard time believing the therapist. Imagine their reaction to her explanation. "This is a child with autism. She just bangs her head till it bleeds all the time. Nothing's wrong. Don't worry. I'm taking her back to the institution."

It sounds a little far-fetched to the average person, doesn't it? But with some education the police might have realized sooner that this does occur. Instead they started questioning the girl, and the situation escalated as she began cursing. Obviously, there are all types of scenarios in which emergency responders can find themselves. Complicate that with a subject at the scene who has autism, and you're in a most precarious situation. How do you handle challenging circumstances without escalating them further?

Do not make this a contest

If I could create one big philosophy for handling encounters with persons who have autism it would be based on understanding. I want to avoid those disgusted, aggravated looks from people who don't know what the disorder really is. That look of disdain is horrifying to me because they're not even giving themselves a chance to understand. I want to avoid needless confrontations. For example, a police officer may tell a guy with autism to stand still, but the guy is unable to stop rocking. I hate to see an ensuing scene where the officer then yells, "I said stand here!" The guy continues to move, and things escalate from there. "What did I say to you?!"

Especially for policemen, I urge over and over again that this is not a contest between you and the person with autism. This is not someone belligerent because he doesn't obey your commands. Please don't fall into that swat-like mentality that says, "We're here to enforce what we know is right, and we will do it by any means necessary because we are the right guys. We are the good guys. You are the bad guys. You're not like us. It's us against you." That mentality is what puts my son at risk – at risk of being injured or possibly killed in a confrontation.

I notice a lot of people get excited with power when they see weakness. I'm asking you to get that power rush out of your system. These people are not prey. They're not to be picked on. My son's fears, behaviors, and inability to get into his life are not his fault. It doesn't mean he's weak. It simply means he has a lot of other problems to overcome first. You have to quell that need to overpower a person who has a weakness you think is stupid. Have some sympathy and understanding. You don't need a lot of training to have a heart.

Escalated behavior

You may find a person with autism already in an agitated state when you get to the scene. You get there and you find someone pacing back and forth hitting herself in the head repetitively. What probably happened? Maybe a light or smell suddenly overwhelmed her. She may then have started to act out by pacing, having a small seizure, or by hitting herself. So somebody may then have said, "Hey, you can't do that in here. Hey! I said you can't do that in here." People start looking at her and yelling more at her, and the behavior continues to escalate. Or maybe she was accused of stealing and the storekeeper locked her in.

The way you approach the person at the scene may also cause escalated behavior. Direct questioning, body posture, and insistence on an answer can cause behavior escalation. Let's say you were called because a well-built, twelve-year-old blond boy wearing a high school jacket is taking merchandise and putting it all over the store. He's not listening to the store owner and he won't leave. So you come at him and tap him sternly on the shoulder. "Hey, come here a minute!" The boy now starts doing repetitive actions, turns away, covers his ears, starts rocking back and forth or walking uneasily.

Escalated behavior is like a flight or fight response. I hate to put it this way, but imagine putting an animal from the zoo into mid-town Manhattan. All the traffic and noises assault it. Obviously it has no idea what's going on and starts to panic. So it starts to run, stampede, or attack because it's very confused. Almost the same holds true for a person with autism. If the situation is pushed the wrong way everything becomes heightened. Everything becomes too much. He starts pacing back and forth, back and forth. And you say, "Hey, I'm talking to you." And the more you do that, the more he goes away.

This is a very particular response that should signal there's something amiss here. This is not a criminal; this is somebody with a problem. I'm hoping you recognize the problem as autism, and not the behavior of a criminal.

People with autism, although seemingly normal, don't have behavioral issues. They are not psychologically ill or bad people. It's their disorder that causes behavioral outbursts. If a kid fell down because she had severe muscle spasticity from cerebral palsy, would you say to her, "I said get up and walk!" No. You'd say, "The kid's got a disability. Let's help her... Do you use a wheelchair? Do you need crutches? Are you hurt? Can I help you?" You'd be so into helping this kid, and so calm and so feeling for her. Picture asking my son a question. He runs back and forth, and grits his teeth, tries to bite, smacks his hands, hits himself in the head, and twirls around. I don't want you to stand there and say, "What's the story with this guy?" I want you to say the same thing, "Okay, take it easy. Come here. Are you okay? Come here." Don't discriminate against him because you don't recognize his disorder.

You need to realize that the boy at the store looks a little off; something's wrong here. You've got to differentiate between the escalated behavior of autism and the escalated behavior of somebody who is belligerent or on drugs. I hope that bell in your head will ring and you'll know to step back, not touch him again, give him his space and quiet, and get that eye contact. Maybe you'll tell everybody in the store to back off. Do you have a space in the back? Do you have a stock room we can go to? It may be hard to get him there, but clear that store. Tell that clerk who's mad to go back to work and leave you alone with him. Make a quiet space for yourself.

Although a person with autism may exhibit aggressive, belligerent, evasive, and other guilty-looking behaviors, he really is very different from a criminal or person on drugs. Criminals talk about themselves. They use emotion, facial expressions, and direct the conversation toward you or them. They are not repetitive, and if they come up close to you, it's with a puffed-up attitude. "You're saying I stole this? Is that what you're saying?" Whereas if you ask a kid with autism, "Did you take that candy bar?" he'll answer repetitively with no emotion. "Yes, yes, yes, yes, yes." You have to say to yourself, "I don't think she means yes. I don't know what she means." When someone answers, "No, officer, I was just standing here," that can look guilty and evasive. But if he answers, "No, no, no," and he starts moving his fingers, then you should rethink the situation. Training and awareness are important, but if you have a spark of humanity in these situations an alarm should go off anyway.

A criminal wouldn't have that fight or flight look. He would more likely be trying very hard to look innocent. "What's going on here?" "Nothing, officer. Just standing around." Notice though, that he makes sense. He's lucid and he's talking to you. He might come up close to you and respond. "Why are you asking me? Why don't you back off?" If you ask, "What happened here?" to the person with autism she might turn away and start twiddling her fingers or flapping her hands. And the more you ask questions, the more the actions escalate. So that should signal to you, "Okay, put your adrenaline down. This is a different person. Back off. Quiet down. Slow down your body language." That's the best help you can give this person.

What if you're called to a store where a guy's throwing CD cases all over yelling, "Fuck you! Don't tell me what to do!" As a police officer your reaction would be, "Hey, come over here. That's it. Turn around. Let me put the cuffs on you." See that he under-stands what he's saying, and is belligerently acting with emotion. That's very different from arriving to find a guy repetitively smacking himself, a sure sign of autism. You might also have to talk to him several times before he responds. If an eight-year-old boy was screaming because he was upset, you'd say, "Calm down." Most likely you'll be able to see that he was listening to you. A child with autism, however, might not calm down no matter what you said because you might not reach him. You can see that difference and make the assessment that this is a person with autism, not a criminal.

Handling aggression or dangerous behaviors

Let's take a person who is hurting himself or is violent, aggressive, or potentially dangerous to you and others. No question you have to stop it. Realize when approaching a person with autism that this is a special situation. Typically, if you came upon a girl banging her head until it bled, your instincts would tell you to cuff her now, throw her in the wagon, and send her to the asylum. But with your better awareness, you can now assess that she has a disability that is probably autism. So forget your normal reactions and try gently to stop her.

What do you do if she turns around and attacks you? Number one, keep yourself from getting hurt. Restrain her. The method most used is to come from behind. Usually teachers will use a wraparound method where you come from behind and wrap around with your arms, enveloping the child. You contain her very gently, almost like a strait-jacket, until she calms down. You should also be very calming in your voice, "Okay, take it easy. Okay." You can feel the aggression go out of her.

I've had to wrap my arms around my son and put him in a hold because he was hitting his head. The next minute he calmed down and was kissing me. Wrapping your arms around the child is less confrontational than grabbing him or her from the front. And don't forget to repeat a very gentle, "Okay, calm down." You're not throwing him to the ground. You're not punching him. If he goes to bite you, try to get out of the way and put your arms around him to calm him down. Say, "Okay, honey, take deep breaths." Then try again. In most cases you can make the situation manageable if you use a little common sense and a little kindness. You don't need to jump on him right away. This is not a violent criminal.

This is a person who is acting violently because of a disorder. That's quite different from arriving at a scene with a big guy on speed and beer who says, "Get the hell away from me," and pushes you and jumps on you and throws a punch. My son has a disorder. Whether you like it or not, this disorder will sometimes erupt in violent and aggressive behavior. Am I excusing it and saying you should get hurt and it's okay? No. But the reality is that it might happen, and you should understand that it's not a decision he consciously makes. It is not a psychological condition or something he can help.

Taking into custody

There might be a few instances when you have to take a person with autism into custody. Maybe he has no ID and you don't know who the parents are. Maybe he's self-injurious or stole something. How about this scenario? You were called to a store where a teenager was acting strangely. The boy looked as if he was refusing to pay attention and when you went to grab him, he bit you. At the time, you didn't know he had autism.

After further investigation you learn of his disorder, but unfortunately, the law says he has committed a crime. He attacked you and you're going to have to cuff him and take him into custody. Please, don't throw him in jail, general lock-up, or the holding cell! That's the worst thing. Number one, he could hurt himself or others. Also, people with autism don't understand what's going on and are the easiest prey in the whole world. People can and have taken advantage of them very easily. So keep him out of harm's way until you sort this out.

It is very important now that you try to segregate him as much as possible. If he's violent or aggressive he may need to be restrained, but keep him isolated. You're going to have to find a quiet spot where you can keep an eye on him and get him calm. Usually there's an office, perhaps the roll call room. Dim the lights and remove any odors that may upset him. As you get him in calmer surroundings you should be using calmer speech and actions. Don't bombard him with questions. Be sure to give him any item he may have been carrying. That might be all he needs to calm down. "Relax. Here's the ball you were carrying. You can have this." Possibly there will be a change.

Have someone keep an eye on him because you don't want him to run or hurt himself. Try to get in touch with parents or a guardian who will know how to handle this, but if you can't, contact the local chapter of the Autism Society of America or the person who trained you. They can guide you through the encounter. Take all these steps first before you act further on a criminal activity. Don't press charges for stealing if the boy has autism. He didn't purposely go out and steal; there's an explanation here. He has a disability that causes uncontrollable impulsive behaviors. Send him home with his parents or guardian. And be sure to talk to them so this kind of situation is prevented in the future.

Conscious participation in a crime?

It's pretty unusual for a person with autism to be involved in a serious crime. Most are not actively participating in the outside world. Some, however, are capable of functioning in society and holding a job. Unfortunately, there are instances when somebody decides to take advantage of them. Problems also occur when a teenager isn't carefully monitored by his parents. It is easy to take advantage of people with autism because they are very compliant. They will do what they're told, take statements literally, and do not question. "We're going to leave the office and you keep your eye on our coats." The person with autism will go stand right by the coats.

Cases of autistics unwittingly tricked into committing crimes have been reported. People have taken advantage of them by telling them to do something illegal: "On your way home there's a package sitting on the desk. Bring it to my house." "Okay." The package turns out to be full of money or illegal contraband. Let's say my son has a job and the person in the office says, "Do me a favor. Go into Mr Arthur's office, take his briefcase, and bring it to me." It turns out the briefcase has jewels in it. My son would just comply without any realization of what he's done.

There have been instances in which street criminals have used kids with autism to deliver drugs. "Take this package to so and so." The kid does it without any idea of what he's doing. He was simply told to do it. When questioned, a real criminal will say, "He told me to do it. I didn't know." The person with autism will answer, "Yes." "Why'd you take it?" "Yes." There's a clear-cut difference in the responses and you should see quickly that this is somebody being taken advantage of because of a disability.

You need to understand how easily people with autism can be manipulated.

Routine traffic stops may not be so routine

When a person with autism travels in a car she depends on an uninterrupted trip. If things go awry, she may easily become upset, aggressive, self-injurious, or try to flee the car. If you pull over a family with an autistic child during a routine traffic stop, be prepared for what may appear to you as a lack of cooperation by the driver. It may just be a need to protect the child from the interruption rather than disrespect for you. Stopping the engine, a stranger approaching the car, flashing lights and sirens, the driver exiting the car are all typical things that can trigger autistic behaviors. Please understand and respect the driver's wishes to stay in the car or keep the motor running to avoid further problems. There have been incidents when trips have been interrupted by routine traffic stops and the children in the car have banged their heads through the window, attacked the driver when the engine stopped, and had epileptic seizures triggered by the flashing lights.

CHALLENGING CIRUCUMSTANCES – AN OVERVIEW

- Remember that a person with autism may be traveling with a therapist or aide who is not necessarily trained or equipped to handle emergency situations.

- Do not make this a contest. Avoid needless confrontation.

- Differentiate between escalated behavior of autism and escalated behavior of drugs or antisocial attitudes.

- Restrain or arrest only as last resort.

- If restrained or arrested, segregate and call parents, contact person, or expert immediately.

- Assess whether the person understands he has committed a crime. A person with autism is very unlikely to comprehend that his compulsive behavior is illegal.

- May have extreme food and drug allergies.

- A person with autism may not understand that a crime against her such as robbery or rape has been committed; she may not know how to report it.

- The most seemingly trivial request by a parent should not be ignored. It may make the difference to having a positive or negative encounter.

Chapter 7

Particular Challenges for Ambulance and Emergency Room Workers

If called to an accident, how do you determine whether a person has autism or whether a person with autism is hurt? First, survey the individual for weak self-help skills and lack of communication. If he says he's "Okay, nothing happened," or "I don't know," you had better take a good look. It probably means he has a mental disability. I always stress evaluate, evaluate, and reevaluate. If a person with autism is sitting in a car wreck he may not even have understood that he was in a wreck! He may just defer the whole incident so that it's gone from his reality. Perhaps he has a very high threshold of pain. He might not know he's hurt, might not tell you, or might not think it's important. He may not recognize danger, pain, or that the person he's with is hurt. In fact, he may be absorbed in watching a tree right now. All these are very protective autistic responses to shield himself from over-stimulation.

A serious problem can be very minor to a person with autism. But a minor scrape can be traumatic. When my son scraped his leg he had to be in sweat pants for three days because he couldn't deal with seeing it. He paced the floor and looked at it constantly. It was very serious to him.

Evaluating for injury

So how do paramedics or emergency room workers evaluate for injury? The most important thing is first to win the victim over with quiet coaxing and repetitive sentences. "Look at me. Look at me." Explain as minimally as you can what you're going to do, one step at a time, and demonstrate on yourself or a co-worker. "I'm just going to touch your arm. See. Doesn't hurt. Just going to touch your arm." You want to win their confidence so you can do a full body check.

Good emergency workers go up to a typical child and quietly say, "Hi buddy. I'm here to help you." They immediately slow themselves down because when approaching children, the best way is not to rush at them. Approach a child with autism the same way, but you might have to use a little extra coaxing and repetitive speaking and a little less explanation. Cut your words a bit and repeat them several times. Show the basics. Leave out the details. Details are unnecessary. Keep everything short, direct, calm, quiet, and repetitive. I urge you to try as hard as possible in a terrible emergency to be as gentle and understanding as possible.

What if you need to approach a child in a car who's injured and bleeding? You might say, "Okay, I'm going to come in and sit next to you now." Now the child turns away and starts to shake his head because he can't deal with the situation. You're going to try again, but you're not going to stop his head from moving. That's his repetitive behavior, and there's no need to stop it unless he's banging and hurting himself. Don't take that head shaking for lack of understanding or not trying. This might be his way of comforting himself. So ignore the behavior and get his attention by repeating, "Honey, look at me. Can you look at me? Okay. Good. Very good. I'm going to come in and just look at your arm. Look at your arm."

You might have to get in there no matter what if time's running out and you see there's injury or a chance of internal injury. "I see his arm is bleeding, I can't wait any longer, and he's not responding. if I don't get him to the hospital he's going to lose a lot of blood." Very quietly take control, survey the body, and get him to the hospital.

Administering medication

Kids with autism are often on many different medications and are prone to allergic reactions or dangerous drug interactions. That is why it is probably a better choice not to administer any medications to a patient with autism unless it is an absolute necessity.

Gaining cooperation in the emergency room

If as an emergency room worker you've established the patient has autism, admit her as quickly as possible. It's not that she's more important than the other people waiting. It's just that a part of her disorder is that she can't wait. Waiting and fearing the unknown bring stress levels up and up and up. Before long the person will be out of control and almost impossible to treat. Try to take a person with autism to the quietest place in the emergency room, block out noise, and turn the lights off if you can. If parents are there, don't pass off the little things they request as trivial. Asking to dim the lights, for instance, is not silly. Bright lights can be very upsetting to someone with autism.

Next try to explain what's going to happen. Speak very quietly and directly. That doesn't mean to talk a lot or in great depth. The more you talk at the patient, the more she's going to tune out and become agitated. In other words, don't speak all the time. Just give the briefest details and leave her alone. She'll be fine if you let her relax a bit. If possible, explain visually. I know that's hard in an emergency situation because you can't draw pictures, but just explaining the way you would to a typical child won't work. You have to try to show them. Demonstrate in a quiet, simple manner. Let's say you need to take the child's blood pressure. Don't say, "I'm going to take your blood pressure now with this machine. The blood pressure's going to measure how high… Look it can go up to 80…" You've lost her.

What you want to do is demonstrate on yourself, a colleague, or a parent and say, "We're going to bring you over to this machine. And watch, I'm just going to put this band on you, and then it will be over quickly. I promise. See, the band's on me, and now I'm going to put it on you." That's the best way to do it. You've spoken in very simple, short, direct phrases and you've shown the child what's going to happen. If she's still upset and not responding, repeat it again. "Honey, watch me. Can you look over here? Just look at me. I'm going to take this band and put it on you. Like this. And then it will be off in a minute. Real quick. Okay, let's do it. Can we do it now? Let's do it." It is very likely that a person with autism will be so nervous that she's practically jumping out of her skin. Realize that. This is a person who doesn't fit in with the norm, so try to use extra effort and understanding to help her.

Even walking through doors can be a major dilemma. In the child's mind, all he knows may be, "I can't go through these doors. I just can't do it." Just saying to him, "Come on. We have to go in. It's okay. I'm not going to hurt you," won't work with a kid with autism. Find another route. If that's not possible, then coax him through those doors as quietly as you can. Say, "We're going to do this. We can do this together. Now all we're going to do is push open this door and walk through, and it's going to be real quick. I'll show you. We can do it. Come on, here we go." And take the child step by step.

If the child is not responding a time may come when you have to use what's classified as a physical prompt. Put your hands on his shoulders and say, "Come on. We're going to do this." And keep nudging him toward the door. Unfortunately, even this may not work and the time may come when you have to say, "It's urgent we get him in there," or "I've got 300 other patients. And I hate to say it, but if I don't get him in and examine him now, he's going to wait for three hours." You're going to have to take the child by the hand or put your hand on his shoulder and gently prompt him. I will also state unequivocally that there might come a time when you have to restrain, carry, or strap the child to a gurney. I hate to see that happen, but I understand it.

> We had responded to an EMS call at Bill Davis' home, and I think that may have actually sparked his idea that he should start training paramedics about autism. So he came out and trained us on what we should look for when we arrive on the scene with a child with autism. It's probably the first time we ever had anybody talk to us about it and it was a very informative session. He stressed that people with this disorder are not mentally retarded or crazy, and schooled the staff on what types of problems children with autism have. The staff all felt that it was beneficial.
>
> We don't really run into many people with autism. In fact, probably none of the staff in our department knew anything about it before the training. Unless we run into it on a daily basis, it's really not something that we know about, and also why we might not be prepared to handle it well without some training. I certainly would recommend that all EMS departments get training like this and that it should be done on a yearly basis for everyone to keep updated. (Mike Fitzgibbons, Executive Director, Susquehanna Valley Emergency Medical Services)
>
> There was an editorial in the paper about another hospital's emergency department visit by a child with autism and

how poorly that staff handled it. So Bill Davis called every emergency department in Lancaster County to arrange talks to them about the disorder. I agreed to have him come because any education is great. After all, that editorial incident could have been our department and training is a good preventative.

Registered nurses, support techs, and unit clerks all attended Bill's talks. I think it was very beneficial because the staff had a lot of questions for him. What made it so good was that he personalized it. He related stories about his son and put a face to the disorder. The staff was really impressed. They may have known about the disorder, but by personalizing it they could see it from the family perspective. I think they understand better that it's not the child acting out, but characteristics of the disorder itself. I would recommend this training for all emergency room personnel. My staff really paid attention and enjoyed it. They had a lot of questions for him. (Jolyne Barnett, RN, BSN, CCRN, Nurse Manager, Emergency Department Lancaster General Hospital)

AMBULANCE AND EMERGENCY ROOM CHALLENGES – AN OVERVIEW

○ Assess for injury.

○ Interpretation of pain may be abnormal.

○ Serious injury may be ignored or minor scrapes may be interpreted as traumatic.

○ If parent/caregiver is unable to respond, look for child's ID card or key tag explaining child's disorder.

○ Approach slowly. Be calm, direct, quiet, and repetitive.

○ Ambulance or emergency room settings may be highly over-stimulating, agitating, or even painful. Take child to a quiet place as quickly as possible.

○ Patient may have severe allergies to food and/or drugs.

○ Try to demonstrate on yourself or a colleague when explaining procedures. Use drawings or pictures.

Remember that people with autism may act over-excited or agitated when faced with the unknown or when they don't know what's expected of them.

Chapter 8

Fire Rescue

The big issue for firefighters is usually rescue. How do you rescue a child with autism from a burning building? Remember that people with autism tend to do whatever they can to make themselves feel comfortable, especially in stressful situations. So here's a child in a burning home. It's hot, smoky, chaotic, and there's a very scary-looking firefighter in full gear coming toward him. What's the child going to do? Defer the situation by going to the area in which he feels most comfortable. It could be his room or perhaps a little spot by the TV. Recently triplets, all with autism, died in a house fire. They were each found in the little areas of their home that they liked best. All three crawled deeper and deeper into the house, not to get away from the fire, but to get to the area that they loved. And that's where they died.

Chances are your victim will also find comfort by going deeper inside the house, defeating your efforts at rescue. Unable to deal with what's going on the child goes back to what makes him feel good; what eases his discomfort. "There's a huge fire. I can't conceptualize what's going on. There's someone screaming in a scary outfit. My mother's not here. It's hot. So I'll go to my little doll whose hairs I count, and that will make me feel better. Every time I count it's the same number of hairs and all this other stuff will disappear."

These children tend to go to the room or object that makes them feel comfortable, even with fire. The worst thing for you to do is yell commands or run toward them. The more you run at them, the more apt they are to run away or stay in their comfort zone. That means you have to stay calm in a situation that's not calm. You can't yell, "Don't go there! Get out!" or "Jump out the window!" Quiet, repetitive coaxing is what's required. Determine whether you have time to stop and say gently, "Look at me. Look at me. Come here. Come here." That is the best thing to do. In a heightened time of distress, the more you invade these children's space, the more you come at them, the more you scream at them, the more they retreat. They don't understand your words and feel assaulted.

Picture yourself trapped in a fire in China. A guy comes running up to you screaming in Chinese, but you don't respond because you don't know what he's saying. So he yells at you again because you're not following his directions to go down the stairs. If, however, he came to you, pointed, and very quietly said in Chinese to go down the stairs, you might lean toward where he's pointing. He would then nod his head in agreement and you might get out of there safely.

So if you see a child in the corner flapping his fingers who doesn't seem affected by the fire, make a quick determination that something's wrong here. This child probably has autism or some other developmental disability. If you have any time at all, please try to coax him out to safety. But if not, let your intuition take over. More than likely you're probably going to have to grab him. But try not to yell, "Out of the house!" at the same time. It's probably better at this point for you to grab and say calmly, "You're coming with me." If you yell, "Come on, we're getting out of here!" the child might start inching his way back from you. You could lose him.

I think firefighters have a very different set of circumstances from other emergency responders who may have time to coax the victim quietly into cooperation. Firefighters are in a situation where the person they are trying to save could easily be sent running in the wrong direction. And anything can set a person with autism off, even a cough. Bang! Good-bye. He's up in the attic. If the situation is at all dangerous a firefighter may have to grab the person, rather than risk setting him off with words or actions. When approaching a developmentally disabled person there are times when a quick grab is the only choice for an efficient rescue.

> I think that training for autism and all disabilities is excellent because as a firefighter you deal with all segments of the population, and any information we can learn helps. The biggest advantage is just in knowing how to understand and communicate with a person who has autism. If we know what they're thinking and you know why they're acting or reacting the way they are, it better helps us effectively handle the situation. Sometimes when you deal with all types of people you don't view it correctly. You may think someone is just fooling around because you didn't recognize the fact they have some type of disability that makes it harder for them to communicate effectively. A good example is when people who have diabetes go into diabetic shock they can sometimes seem very similar to somebody who has been consuming alcohol. Without proper training you may jump to the conclusion that this person has been drinking when in fact it's a medical emergency. It's the same situation with autism and other disabilities. The more educated you are, the better you are able to help the public.
>
> I think Bill's training was very, very helpful. I would have to say that the largest percentage of us was not knowledge-

able about autism beforehand. Any time we can get training of this nature it's beneficial, and his training was certainly beneficial to us. (Battalion Chief Duane Hagelgans, Battalion C, Lancaster City Bureau Of Fire)

FIRE RESCUE – AN OVERVIEW

- Make quick determination whether occupant has autism or other developmental disability (See Chapter 3, Characteristics of Autism).

- Look for window sticker denoting child with autism is an occupant. "Unlocking Autism" is now selling 'Child with Autism' decals for your bedroom windows. Contact:

  Shelley Reynolds at 225-938-8564 or email Keys2UA@aol.com

- Always remember: people with autism will gravitate to places of comfort or "quiet" during times of stress or danger. These places may include:
  - Their bedroom
  - Attic
  - Crawl space
  - TV room
  - Closets
  - Corners
  - Under beds

- When a person with autism is encountered, she may unexpectedly move away from you to seek comfort despite heat, fire or noise. Children with autism are capable of blocking out disturbing or dangerous situations.

- ○ If it is determined that a person with autism lives in the home and you don't see her immediately, she may have already gone to a place of comfort. The fire truck and loud sirens may have already scared her off:
  - ○ Keep calm
  - ○ Don't shout commands
  - ○ No rapid waving or pointing
  - ○ Use short, repetitive requests

In heightened times of stress, the more you invade the space of an autistic person or shout commands at them, the more likely they are to retreat.

- ○ If you are unsuccessful in gaining the child's attention (she is flapping, rocking, avoiding eye contact, moving away, etc.), grab and rescue! Don't risk retreat.

- ○ After rescue, try to bring the autistic child to the quietest place possible, reunite with parents, and explain that the situation is over. A fire truck is probably not the best place to have a child sit. It is too overwhelming.

- ○ Check carefully for injuries and burns. People with autism may defer sensations of pain.

Reminder! A firefighter's appearance can be very frightening.

Chapter 9

Shoplifting and Store Disturbances: A Special Problem for Retailers and Law Enforcement Officers

A common call to police relating to people with autism concerns shoplifting and public disturbance. There are many instances when an autistic child is believed to be shoplifting or running out of the store with merchandise. Autism's peculiar behaviors can also be misconstrued as vandalism or plotting to steal. The disorder's impulsive behaviors are also often seen as disruptive. My son, for instance, is disruptive each time he impulsively pushes through a line of people. He's pushed to the front of a line on a number of occasions when the urge to get what he desires is very great. Waiting causes him such anxiety that he loses all self-control.

Another impulsive behavior my son has that can create a store disturbance is rearranging things according to a pattern. Putting objects in ordered patterns is very typical autistic behavior. He may start rearranging movies in a video store by color or title. He may take videos and put them behind others either because he doesn't want to see them or he's hiding them to buy later. He might go into a music store and rearrange CDs. "I want this blue one over here, this red one over there." Focused only on his need to order the CDs, you would see him marching back and forth, holding things, putting them back, taking them out, putting them back, taking them out, putting them over here... If I was a clerk I'd say to myself, "Watch this guy. He's getting ready to do something."

Even though we've taught Chris that before he buys a movie video he must wait on line and pay, he sometimes gets so over-stimulated wanting this movie that he can't control himself. He has a whole ritual when he gets a new movie that is almost impossible for him to delay. First he scrapes off the barcode, opens the package, throws the plastic in the garbage, takes out the video, and reads the cover. Then he has to put the cover underneath the video and carry it a certain way.

This ritual is so strong a force within him that he can't help himself. "I've got to get this out. I've got to open it up, and then I've got to stack it like this. I've got to get home now and put it with my other movies." I've stood in line with him at the movie store, and his legs start to go. He quivers because he can't wait. This overwhelming ritualistic desire makes him happy; but it also rules his behavior. Imagine the store clerk's reaction when Chris wanders up to the front of the store with a couple of movies, starts scraping off the barcode, and takes them out of the package while I'm in the back of the store. "Is this guy trying to rip off those videos?"

If I tell Chris he can buy only one movie and he sees a second one that he wants he will start scraping the barcode and plastic off anyway. He looks at me as if to say, "Okay, you have to pay for it now because it's open." In his mind it's his now because it's open. If Chris is really intent on getting something he will start to shake – he needs that movie! If I say he can't have it he shakes and screams. He has an overwhelming desire to get that movie, rip up the cover, and put it in certain places. I fear that one day when he is a teenager and knows to pay and not to steal, this force could still hit him and he would walk out with the movie if he didn't have the money or couldn't stand on line.

Let's say we give Chris a chance to buy his own movie, and he's very excited. He sees two movies that he wants. He's on a long line, starts scraping off the barcode, and runs out of the store. Hands are flapping, he's running, and now you've got somebody who in actuality did shoplift. The store clerk yells after him, "Hey, what are you doing?"

What happened? He was so intent on getting those movies that he deferred everything else. "I know I have to pay, but right now the most important thing is this red wrapper. I must have this and put it on my wall. Goodbye. I'm moving now. I'm not doing anything wrong because I must have this. Every neuron is telling me that I need this. I'm focused just on this red wrapper, and I'm taking it. I didn't make a decision to steal it. I have to take it. And I can't hear anybody telling me to stop. And I'm getting out of here because everybody's coming at me."

No question this is thievery. But please, step back and say to yourself first, "Am I seeing the behavior of a shoplifter or somebody with some type of disability? There's something a little off here. A shoplifter would be hiding something. Here's a person who looks anxious, is doing some nervous finger play, and he's walking away with something right in front of me. It doesn't all fit."

When it doesn't all fit, you might have a situation with a person who has a mental disability. If somebody comes in drunk or disruptive and they rip up the movies, then you say, "Uh oh. We're in trouble." But when somebody looks strange and is doing repetitive behaviors or looks completely tuned out, think to yourself for a minute: "Is this somebody who is mentally ill or disabled? Is this somebody with some type of problem that he can't help? Am I seeing something that I should be sympathetic towards?" Don't pounce on this person. Don't readily assume that he's a thief, a conman, or on drugs. Think a little bit.

If you're a retailer and you do call the authorities, let them know what you think. "I have somebody here who is taking all my movies off the shelves. But I think the person needs help. So take it easy." That would be the best thing you could possibly do. Help my child and others like him with autism by having some sympathy. You don't need to be an overly-trained store clerk or law enforcement officer to have a heart.

SHOPLIFTING – AN OVERVIEW

A person with autism may not be aware that they have committed a crime. So-called "criminal" behavior may only be satisfying their obsessive need for an object. Without even thinking of paying they may grab objects such as candy bars, CDs, or dolls. The following behaviors are usually uncontrollable:

- Rearranges or lines up objects, puts objects in patterns, rips books or papers
- Leaves store holding and transfixed on object without paying for it
- Is unable to wait on line
- Appears very nervous and agitated (resembling shoplifter)
- Walks through store in robotic-like path; following a specific route can be very important
- Stares at displays or lights
- Opens and closes doors
- Turns lights on and off
- Pushes customers to get to front of line
- Pushes customers to get to desired object
- Uses clothing on racks as a towel
- Incessantly smells objects
- Marks objects he likes or wants with spit
- People with autism are very compliant; a thief may have instructed them to go into a store and bring out a specific object.

If you must arrest or detain an autistic person:

- Contact parents
- Keep segregated
- Keep in a quiet, comfortable space.

Remember: this type of behavior is not a psychological condition. It is neurological.

Chapter 10

How Emergency Responders and Parents can Work Together

Emergency responders and parents working together can make the community more aware of autism. By doing so, they will make each of their jobs easier. Here is a list of what emergency responders can do with parents of children who have autism:

1. Keep a computer list of children with autism in your jurisdiction. Contact pediatricians, local autism support groups, known families and advocates with autistic children. Ask them to have families with autism register with local emergency responders. If possible, provide a form that can be copied and used for registration. Be sure to include behavioral descriptions such as: nonverbal, biter, runner, aggressive, head-banger, etc.

2. Keep autism contact numbers handy (local autism support groups and local advocates).

3. Hold autism awareness days at your station house. Meet and greet parents and children. Show equipment. Ask what parents need from you. Ask parents to pass out informational flyers to local retailers.

4. Keep picture cards in station house and vehicles for easy communication with nonverbal children. Picture cards can be used to ask questions or for children to answer questions. The cards can even be used to describe a criminal. Picture cards can be obtained from: Lenore P. Wossidlo, tel: 412-241-4370, email: *lwossidlo@aol.com*

5. Invite autism advocates to speak and give training sessions at roll call or staff meetings.

6. Visit homes of families with autism, if possible, to help each child feel comfortable with you and to get layout of residence. Establish where child's bedroom and comfort spaces are located.

7. Respect the disorder!

An instructional message to parents

Without a doubt, it is important that emergency responders be made knowledgeable about how to effectively handle situations with a person who has autism. But ultimately it is the parent's responsibility to keep their child with autism safe. I believe in 100 per cent parental responsibility. The police are not going to knock on your door and ask if you have a disabled child so they will know to watch out for him. Your neighbors aren't automatically going to know how to react when they see your child acting oddly. It is your responsibility to introduce your child to his community. It is your responsibility to teach your autistic child basic safety rules just as you would a typical child. It is your responsibility to create a safe environment. Here is a list of steps you can take in order to do that:

1. Safety-proof your home

The first step is to make your home a safe haven. As you would in any home with small children, child-proof your house in the traditional manner. Because your child has autism, however, you'll want to take it a few steps further.

2. Install screen doors and alarms

In the beginning our son, Chris, didn't know anything. He wouldn't respond to anything, yet he barely slept. Since he didn't understand to stay in his room at night we feared he would wander out and fall down the steps, run out of the house, go to the kitchen and get a knife, or turn on hot water and burn himself. It was terrible. We couldn't get any sleep, but locking him in the room seemed as if we were treating him like an animal. He couldn't see or be in touch with us, especially during the day, and we couldn't see or hear him.

So my ever-creative wife, Jae, replaced Chris's bedroom door with a screen door. It was perfect! He loved it. He now had access to the world, but we could also lock his door and still know what he was doing. The biggest safety bonus was that when Chris woke up in the middle of the night he could no longer run out! I know there are also monitor systems, but this worked very well for us. It seemed so much less restrictive than a solid door.

We also put a screen door on our front entrance. Chris loves to look outside, a common trait of kids with autism. So we installed a screen door with a good lock so that he can enjoy the fresh air and watch the kids outside without running out of the house. We've also taught him to open the door in case of emergency or if we get locked out. I can say, "Open door," and he'll open it for Daddy and then go back to his movie. Sometimes he'll open the door and actually feel the breeze, but then he closes and locks it.

One of the new things people are doing to know if their child has run out of the house is to install alarms on doors that sound if the door is opened. You can put on 12 locks and some of these kids can still open them and get out. When the alarm sounds, however, you know if your child has opened the door. Your neighbors, too, will know if they hear the alarm that they should look out for your child.

3. Use emergency alert decals

Another way to make your home safe is with emergency alert decals. Start with a decal for firefighters that alerts them to the fact that a child with autism is in a particular room. The local Illinois chapter of the Autism Society of America sells these for about $1.50 each. They are brightly colored and read: "EMERGENCY ALERT… Occupant with Autism… may not respond to verbal command." You can write to them at the Autism Society of Illinois, 2200 South Main St, Suite 317, Lombard, IL60148-5366, tel: 630-691-1270, (see Appendix A).

I also have a decal for one for my cars that says "Emergency notice – person with autism on board." It alerts others that there's a person with autism in the car if you're in an accident and lists behavior characteristics like "may not respond" and "may be non-verbal."

4. Carry an autism emergency ID card

You should also carry an autism ID card with you in case you're in an accident and unable to communicate. You need to be sure that people on the scene will know how to approach your child. The card should have behavioral information like nonverbal autistic, echolalic, bites, runs, spits, self-injurious, or Down's syndrome autistic. Choose whatever is most important for strangers to know when approaching your child. Our son's ID says "nonverbal autistic." Also don't forget to include your updated telephone number and address, contact persons, and important allergies. Carry the laminated ID in your wallet with your license or hang it with your keys. That way when the emergency workers look for your ID they will also see your child's ID and immediately know that he has autism and what his unique disabilities and behaviors are. If you cannot find a retail store that makes custom laminated cards, then you can easily make your own by following our simple instructions in Appendix B. We also have the instructions posted on our website at http://www.breaking-autisms-barriers.com.

5. Have your child wear an Emergency ID tag

In addition to the emergency ID card, get a number of ID tags and have your child always wear one. One of the first actions we took to protect Chris was placing a little emergency ID tag around his neck. This helps identify him if he is ever in an emergency situation. If he were to run or we lost track of him, this tag would help strangers identify and communicate with him. When someone approaches a child wearing one of these tags they will see it and immediately know he has autism, what characteristics to expect, and who to contact for help.

But what if your child cannot tolerate a tag hanging on his neck or wrist? Chris hated wearing his. So Jae came up with an ID tag that's attached to the shoe with the shoelace. These bright, silver tags are attached to the shoelace and are quickly noticed by helping professionals like police officers and firefighters. Chris had no trouble with this ID because placement on the shoe prevented tactile discomfort. It also prevented removal. If your child has a shoe ID tag make sure you have a few of them and check to see that one is always on the shoe. The tags should include vital information like your child's name, phone number, address, behavioral characteristics, and contacts. You can have tags made at most jewelry counters or in machines at stores like Walmart for under $10.

6. Give your child a form of communication

Another very important step is to find your child an effective form of communication. It could very well save her life. Don't worry about what you choose as long as it works. It could be as simple as a little sticker carried around that says "help" or a more sophisticated PECS book, computer, or signboard. Anything at all that your child can use to communicate with the world is great.

The form you choose will enable her to answer questions, ask for help, or tell where she lives. We created a PECS book specifically for emergency situations for Chris that we call his Communications Safety Book. If no one else is able to talk for him it allows him to communicate with others. It has social questions such as "Who is your sister?", "Where do you live?" and "What's your phone number?". If you ask my son enough times and get him to listen, he'll give you our phone number by displaying the picture of a phone with the number printed underneath. He can tell if he's hurt, doesn't feel well, or has to go to the bathroom, with the communications book.

For your child to use the book you have to teach her how to answer each individual question through repetition and Discrete Trial format. You also need to teach her who will be asking the questions. That way she's prepared to answer potentially scary strangers like policemen, firefighters, and doctors.

We make sure our son always has his Communications Safety Book with him, and we also carry one in the car trunk as back-up. If you would like to make a safety book like ours, detailed instructions are in Appendix C. It's important that your child always has her chosen form of communication. Communication for your child is such an important step not only for safety. It will reduce her frustration and give her a portal to the world.

7. *Knock on your neighbors' doors*

Introducing yourself and your child to everyone possible is another step for parents. Start out from the smallest point, your neighborhood, and then spread out. Introduce yourself to neighbors, kids on the block, the local pool, and local park workers and tell them about your child. Maybe you can prepare a little pamphlet or flyer to give out with information about both your child and autism.

Explain what autism is and then list the behaviors that would strike people as odd so they don't call the police. For instance, my son has a tendency to pee wherever he is; a lot of kids with autism do. So I explain that if they see him peeing on their front lawn, please don't get upset. Call me and I'll get him. I might explain that my son may go over and pick their flowers. Forgive him. He doesn't know any better. If you see my son running down the street, please call us and follow him because he tends to run. Or maybe a neighbor has a dog. My son is terribly afraid of dogs. Please, if you see him come by could you put the dog inside? And if he reacts terribly, understand that reassuring him, "It's okay. He doesn't bite," is not going to work.

Remember to touch upon your child's strengths as well. You want to humanize him. We don't just say, "This is Christopher and he flaps his hands." We also say "Christopher spells 200 words, he's good at gymnastics, he's playful, he's smart, he uses a computer, and he teaches himself." So people get a view of his humanity, his skills, and his strengths as well as his needs. I never say weaknesses. He has needs. He has needs for visual cues and for quiet speaking. To me that's not a weakness. He's just different.

8. Introduce your child in public places you frequent

Next branch out to local stores you and your child frequent. Everybody knows my son in our mall. When Chris stands on line and pays, the clerks say to him, "Good job, Chris. How are you? Did you get your lizards? Okay, bye-bye." And he responds, "Bye-bye." Now if he picks up an object and forgets for whatever reason to pay for it these people won't run and tackle him or call the police because they know him. Instead they'd call me if I hadn't noticed. They wouldn't be thinking, "Oh, my God, that kid just stole something." They'd be saying, "Bill, Chris just walked out with an object." That's why it's important everybody knows him.

If you go on vacation remember also to tell the front desk that your child has autism. Explain that they might see him do some strange behavioral things. Of course you're always going to get stares, but if you keep the staff informed you're likely to avert any trouble.

9. Hold an Awareness Day

Awareness days are another very effective way to inform your community about autism and your child. Our first awareness day was a barbecue. We announced it in the local paper's calendar and advertised it with flyers. At the barbecue we gave out pamphlets and other informational items about autism that we got from our local Autism Society of America chapter. If you're unable to get any hand-outs from local groups then write something simple yourself. We also had little hand-outs about Chris and what he liked to do. Naturally we have Chris at our awareness days for people to meet, and you'll want your child at your event also.

I think awareness days are very important. They can be done in many ways and as creatively as possible. You can hold awareness days at your house or you can rent a hall. You may know somebody who owns a movie theater. So see if they'll let you put a table in the lobby and hand out pamphlets. All you're really doing is getting some material to hand out, introducing your family, and talking to people. People enjoy learning and they're likely to enjoy whatever it is you do.

Invite the local police chief. Invite the mayor. Invite the press and your state representative. I called everybody I possibly could either to invite them to our awareness days or just to give them information directly. Any group I thought should be informed or would come, I called. If you really want to take things further, offer food and merchandise. We've had t-shirts printed up for our awareness days that say "I met Chris Davis on 10/10/99" and "The Second Annual Autism Awareness Day for Chris Davis." It was our way of personalizing the event. You can even offer the shirts for purchase and raise funds for your local chapter.

Acquiring the t-shirts isn't really all that difficult either. Start in the community by going to the businessman who produces t-shirts and tell him what you're doing. Ask if he can give you a discount in exchange for your advertising his business at the event. Then be sure to put up a sign that says "Thanks to T-shirt Barn for the t-shirts." Suddenly the community begins to realize, "This awareness stuff makes me look good. Plus I wanted to give a little back anyway." So you start getting more things offered to you and the community is getting more involved. I've gone to local restaurants and asked for food donations. Some say yes. Some say no. I've asked dee-jays, "Can you come a couple hours and play music?" Everybody gets a good feeling out of it. It's a very happy marriage. And the bottom line – they learn. The more they learn the better off and safer your family is. It's as simple as that.

10. Register your child

Another thing to do is go to your local police precinct, fire department, ambulance department, and hospital and register your child on their data banks. Give them some pamphlets about autism and a description of your child, where you live, and your phone number. That way if an emergency situation involving your family arises, they will already be aware of what to expect. Provide them with vital information like: nonverbal autistic, uses pictures, bites, can become aggressive, address, phone number, parents will come right away. Maybe you want to include that your child likes to line up videos. So if the police find him in the video store lining up every movie they'll know how to handle him. When they say, "Hey, you've got to stop that," and he starts flapping they'll be aware of this type of behavior. Be sure they understand that your child's actions are not meant to be belligerent. They need to know that your child doesn't realize he's doing anything wrong.

11. Give training sessions

But don't stop there. How about giving training sessions to your local emergency workers? To arrange training sessions I found that it's as easy as calling up the local training officer of your police department or the persons in charge of the emergency room and paramedic departments. The first people I spoke to wanted to know who I was. So I said, "I'm a dad of a child with autism who lives in your neighborhood. It's important that you know this disorder and I'd like to come and train you." Credentials would have been nice, but most parents don't have credentials. Now I do, but I certainly didn't at first.

So how do you get them to agree in the beginning? Align yourself with a group or support group. Choose a curriculum to follow; for example, this book could be used. Just tell the person in charge, "There's a book called *Breaking Autism's Barriers: A Father's*

Story. It's written by a parent who's led training sessions, and I use his format." It could be as simple as that – although I would definitely add, "I'm not calling because you did anything wrong or because there was an incident or I think you're going to hurt my child. I just want you to recognize some things. Can I do that for you?" I think that will get you in the door.

Once you get your foot in the door to hold a training session, what do you do? My first encounter was pretty scary. I was given two groups of police officers to train in two half-hour sessions. It was six in the morning with 30 cops who probably didn't want to be there because they had to come back for a later shift. They had just listened to a highly qualified person on another subject and now they had to listen to me, a person with no credentials. Seeing a couple of men fall asleep, I sped through my talk. But while taking a break between sessions the lieutenant told me I was doing a great job and I should slow down and talk a little more.

It turned out they knew nothing about this disorder and for the most part were very interested! Being a parent, somebody in the trenches, I had the type of experience that lent itself to practical information. I had something to say that was of use to these guys. I wasn't just talking theories. The officers realize, "I didn't know about autism. This is pretty frightening. If I had encountered this kid before his father spoke I would have thought he was on drugs. I would have thought he was violent and hit him with a club. Certainly I would have tackled, smacked, or cuffed him." Then they say, "Not only am I glad to know this. This is fascinating. And I really am learning something. He's helped me to recognize this stuff and use it as a tool." I liken it to learning about cocaine addiction, what someone looks like high, and the different methods used to approach him.

So suddenly I was instilled with a mission; and so should you be. This is a mission to save your child, to make him safe. These people want to learn. They don't want to be bullied or forced, but they do want to hear what you have to say. So don't go there and preach and talk about theory. They're interested in what they're going to see if they should encounter an autistic person, and how they can help. It's a great thing you can do.

If you just tell them what you know about the disorder itself and how to handle only your own child in these situations, you can't go wrong. That's probably enough. By telling them about the disorder you're waking them up to its existence and usually they're shocked. Then when you tell them how to handle it you're giving them a tool. Most people in the emergency service field are interested in this information. Their first questions to you are usually very basic ones about your family. Where do you live? What does your child look like? What's your phone number? That's very important; they're saying to themselves, "I might encounter this child so I want to know who he is and where he lives." Be glad they're asking; it means they're interested.

Don't forget to thank your participants for taking the training. Get a local business to offer them a discount. Arrange with the local dry cleaning business to let them bring their uniforms for ten per cent off. I acquired theater tickets that I gave to the firefighters and police. Not too many people appreciate your local emergency workers. So it's a nice little thing to do that strengthens the ties within your community.

I am very proud to say that every locale I've trained is now very aware. When you describe how different these children are and how differently they communicate, emergency responders realize right away the need for this presentation. I've heard time and time again, "Boy, we needed to learn about this. This is very important." So you just have to swallow hard, use this book, some other training manual, or something you wrote yourself and go out and do it!

12. Give educational presentations

If your training sessions have been successful why not take them a step further and give educational presentations? Arrange to speak to professional associations for social workers, speech therapists, and occupational therapists. Be sure to include pediatricians too; they are often known to be one of the most unaware groups out there.

Go to colleges and speak to the special education and psychology departments. Offer your availability to speak about autism to the social work, speech and language, and medical schools. Speak to group home workers. Here you'll want to gear your talks to the disorder as a whole. Policemen don't need to know the therapeutic value of applied behavior analysis (ABA), whereas a group home worker or somebody attending a university might like to know exactly what kind of therapies we use. So I will lengthen my talk to include ABA, incidental play, what we do at home, how a child learns, what he needs, and how we set up a classroom for my son.

I have even presented to high schools and elementary schools. Elementary schools are wonderful because you're making young kids aware. What if they see your son in the park? Now they won't make fun of him and might even try to include him. Young children love to learn, and ask more questions than anybody – intelligent questions. So I love the elementary schools. When speaking to high schools you may touch some students deeply enough to spark an interest in the field.

Almost any institute of learning will be receptive to these presentations. Just speak to the individual department head and say, "I'm a parent of a child with autism, I have some knowledge, and have done some speaking. Do you think you can spare an hour for me to speak to some interested students about the disorder?" Of course they're going to say yes. It's very rare that somebody says no. You're not selling anything: all you want to do is give knowledge. How many people are going to turn you down? People love programs and knowledge. And one talk leads to more talks because professors will say to you, "Please call my friend at a neighboring school. He's been wanting to do something like this." It won't be long before you're a well-known resource person in the community.

13. Contact your local newspaper

If public speaking is not your strong suit, there are still other steps you can take to educate the public about autism and ensure your child's safety. Call the local newspaper and ask, "Hey, have you done anything on autism? My child has the disorder and I thought you might like to do a little story on what autism is and how we care for her." Not long after an article is in the paper, people have learned about autism, and they've learned about your child.

14. Educate yourself and get involved

Parents have to empower themselves with knowledge. Read widely and attend conferences. Make yourself as knowledgeable as possible, not only so that you can talk to others, but so that you understand the disorder fully. Seek out your local resources: are there advocacy and support groups for autism? If there are none, you might start a group or get one brought in. Send away for as much information as you can. There are pamphlets on how to set up awareness days, how to set up groups, and how to approach politicians. You will be supplied with material to pass out, and you will also learn where to go if you need support, advocacy or legal advice. A lot of organizations are happy to give out material. The National Information Center for Children and Youth with Disabilities (NICCHY) and the Autism Society of America, for example, have tons of information on autism, educational programming, and political movements. Universities and hospitals have programs with good information also – be creative. The more active you become in these groups, the more empowered you will be; so chair a committee or take on a board position.

15. Make political contacts

What happens if you and your child have a bad encounter? Whom do you call? Who's going to help? Who's behind you? Do you know your state representative's history concerning disabilities? Call your representative, tell him about yourself, and ask what he's done for kids with disabilities. Does he know about a pertinent bill that's pending for autism? Make it known that you're a constituent and this is an issue. I've invited senators and congressmen to my home to demonstrate exactly what we are dealing with on a daily basis. Usually they'll delegate an aide to discuss the situation, but if it's important for you directly to speak to the representative, call every day. "You must have forgotten about me. The paper is writing an article about my son. Should I tell them you're not interested?" That's what I've done – you have to push people to respond sometimes.

16. Carry law enforcement pocket cards

Of course no matter how many training sessions and seminars you give, how many boards you serve on, and how many politicians you get on board, not everyone you meet will understand autism. So there are still other measures you need to take to keep your child safe. As you both venture out into the world it's a good idea to carry law enforcement pocket cards that you can get from local chapters of the Autism Society of America. The Kentucky and Illinois chapters both sell the cards, which quickly explain the disorder, its common behaviors, and how to interact. They say something like, "What you are looking at is an incident with a child who has autism. He may appear violent or out of control."

When might you need such an explanation? Picture yourself in the mall trying to subdue your child as he bites his hand, sticks his fingers in his eye, screams, and frantically shakes his head back and forth. You've now caught a policeman's attention and he's looking suspiciously at you. He comes over and demands an explanation: "What's going on here?" "Officer, my son has autism and these are things that he does." "Are you okay?" asks the officer. And your son starts yelling. Now the policeman is even more suspicious. He thinks, "What kind of stuff is this guy handing me? Maybe he kidnapped this child. The child can't speak so how do I know? And the child's bleeding. This man told me the kid hit his own head on the table? What kind of nonsense is this? Now the kid's flapping around. Maybe he's on drugs."

But if you have a card it helps legitimize your explanation. The police officer will say to himself, "If this person carries these cards around, she must be a concerned parent of a child with autism. This must be the right explanation." So carry a bunch of these wallet-sized law enforcement pocket cards with you at all times to hand out if there's ever an incident.

17. Teach safety procedures to your child

I realize that it takes a long time just to get your child first to sit down and attend. I realize there are countless things you must try to teach. But you must also teach your child safety rules. There's a saying that if you put a twelve-year-old child with autism in the mall with ten dollars, he'll starve to death. They simply don't have the ability to take care of themselves. So whether Chris has his ID tag or not, he still will cross the street without looking and still has the potential to wander away. The tag should not lull us into a false sense of security. We have made it a lifetime safety project diligently to teach Chris how to cross the street, not to leave the house, to stay by us when we shop, how to talk to strangers, how to get help, car safety, and fire safety. There are so many areas to cover. And for all those things a typical child easily learns, you now have to develop instruction programs that are repeated over and over again for your child with autism. One of the areas we practice with our son is asking, "What's your name?" Then we teach him to point to his ID tag. This is certainly a question he'll hear during his life, and he now has an effective way to answer.

Unfortunately, Chris was locked in the car a couple of times and it underscored how important it was for us immediately to teach him how to handle himself in the car. So we started a course of teaching him safety rules through repetition using Discrete Trial. First, Chris was taught to fasten his seat belt. Next we moved on to teach him what red and green lights mean so that he knew when to stay seated and when to exit the car. Learning to lock and unlock the doors was another lesson. This included who to unlock the doors for as well. Before he was taught, my wife once locked him in the car while at the car wash, and he refused to open the door for her. Chris also knows that once he leaves the car he has to wait by the door for us to escort him. Otherwise he may wander away and get hit by a car.

Another lesson we teach our son is based on his numerous visits to the mall. Using a social story we taught him that when he needs help, or Mommy and Daddy are not with him, that he goes to the security office. We run through the entire scene like a drill. We take him to the office and have him point to his ID tag and say, "Help me." But first we knock on that security door and get the staff to participate with us. "My son has autism... We're doing a drill. I'd like you to meet him and was hoping you would join us. Could you please help? He's going to come to you now and say

'Help me' and point to his ID tag. Please read his tag and say, 'Good job! I'll call your parents. Come in.' Thanks."

We also plan on getting a firefighter to visit our house so Chris sees their uniform and learns to cooperate rather than run off to comfort himself. We hope the firefighter will participate by explaining fire in a social story. "The building is burning. Here comes the firefighter!" Then the firefighter will walk in and say, "Come here. Come here." Chris will then learn to go with him rather than run up the stairs to his room and play a movie.

We enact the same sort of lesson with a police officer. "Chris, we're walking outside and playing 'Where's Mommy and Daddy?' The police officer will come to our house and Chris will go up to him and say 'Help me.'" But not only do I script my son, I script the emergency service worker so he also knows what to say: "Oh, are you lost?"

18. Use social stories

Use social stories to teach your child how to handle emergency situations like fire, burglary, blackouts, strangers at the door, telephone calls, someone is injured, and calling 911. Do them to teach safety wherever you can, but be sure to tailor the stories to your child's particular lifestyle. You should continue these stories and drills every week until your child is fully grown. Appendix D has examples of safety social stories that we have created for our own son.

I realize all these safety measures seem endless: there is undoubtedly much to do. But don't get overwhelmed. Take it step by step. You don't have to do it all at once, and you may not have to do all of it. Some of it is probably not important to your child or you. But you are going to have to make him safe, and you are going to have to make the neighborhood aware. It's your job, your responsibility. There's no getting around it. My goal is that I make every day for my son as nice and comfortable and meaningful as I can; that he becomes the best he can be. If he can simply walk through the streets and have a decent day, I've done my job. Keeping him safe will help achieve that goal.

Chapter 11

Preventing Problems
in Everyday Life

Telephone and 911 use

I know the story of a man who had to go away for a business meeting and tried to tell his son with autism to keep in touch by telephone. "I'm going to be in a hotel and you can call me there. Here's the number. Dial and say hello to me." After his meeting, the man went back to his hotel room. The phone rang and it was his son. "Hi, Dad." Then silence and the dial tone. The boy hung up because he took his father literally about saying "hello" and did not understand the basics of telephone use.

For a lot of kids with autism, the telephone has very little meaning to them. Any kind of communication can be difficult, and the phone is just one more confusing method. Telephone use is clearly a safety and awareness issue for people with autism. So my wife, Jae, invented a telephone safety awareness social program. She set up a phone on which Chris could dial different numbers and then reach a recording of the person he was dialing. It was a great way to get him used to dialing numbers. He also learned what the phone was and that you could say things on it. Let's say he tried calling his friend, Jimmy. A recording of Jimmy's mom would come on saying, "Jimmy's not home now. Can you call back later?"

One of the things we wanted to teach Chris was to dial 911 in case of an emergency. First we explained what an emergency was with pictures of fire and other situations. Then we taught him to dial the numbers and say he needed help. It wasn't until the day his VCR broke that we knew for sure he understood the concept. One day while my wife and two therapists were home with Chris his VCR stopped working. The VCR is extremely important to him so it being broken caused him huge upset. Jae and the therapists immediately tried to fix the machine, but were not having much success and Chris anxiously walked out of the room. Finally, it was fixed. "Chris," they called, "we fixed it!"

Happy and relieved, he went back to watching his movie. My wife then went to use the phone, but there was no dial tone. Instead she heard, "Do you need help?"

Jae asked, "Who is this?"

"This is your 911 emergency operator. What's the problem?"

"There's no problem. I didn't dial you."

The operator responded, "I'm showing that according to my chart, from your upstairs bedroom phone someone dialed 911."

"I assure you that no one dialed 911."

"Ma'am, do you need the police? We've hung on the line for ten minutes because it's an open line."

"I'm telling you nobody called. There's only me, my son, and the therapists here."

Then it suddenly dawned on Jae that the phone was moved from its regular spot and that Chris had been in the room. Apparently he had taken very literally that the broken VCR was an emergency and had dialed 911. He just didn't verbalize anything when asked what the emergency was. With her sudden realization Jae asked our son, "Christopher, did you dial 911?" And he started to laugh.

This incident pointed out two interesting things about his disorder and our training. Number one, we were very proud of him because he took an independent step to fix the problem himself because he felt others weren't fixing it. We applauded him and told him he did a great job. Number two, it meant he literally interpreted the broken machine as an emergency. "I have an emergency. They told me to dial 911 so that's what I'm doing."

Of course, now we're working on when really to call and what to say. Kids with autism are very literal thinkers so you have to break down your training to teach them exactly what situations require 911. We will do it through repetition and illustration. Things cannot be made too rigid, and somehow we have to expand Chris's thinking. We have to illustrate what it means to be robbed or when a fire needs to be reported. How does he know the difference between a fire in the fireplace and a room dangerously on fire? This is what we have to teach.

Street safety

I find street safety very important for a number of reasons. Because of their ability to defer and being so preoccupied with whatever they are doing, children with autism can literally wander out into traffic. There have been times that I've had to grab Chris when he was reading a book and started to cross a street. When he gets preoccupied he'll just walk out in the street because he's not paying attention. If he looks across the road and happens to see Elmo in the window he'll start to run that way without ever giving it a second thought.

Also I don't know whether he's conceptualized that cars can do him harm. We have constantly to explain to him that cars are dangerous and must be given attention. Another important reason to teach street safety has to do with the fact that a lot of the kids are runners. Eventually they're going to approach traffic so you hope that with training they're going to look before they cross the street.

We find the mall is a great place to teach street safety. Once Chris learns there, we generalize his lessons all over. Everywhere we go now we take that information and use it with him for crossing the street. The first thing we do is teach Chris to stop at the line where the street begins and the parking lot ends. It is then a real mandatory, "Stop. Look both ways… No, look here too. Are there any cars?" "No car." "No car? Okay, then we can go."

One of the problems we've run into at the mall, especially, is when people see us ready to cross they politely wave us on. Here we are telling him not to cross until the cars pass and they're waving us on! This is quite a stumbling block because we don't know what to tell him. Does he really recognize the gesture? Rather than risk it, I'll just wave the cars on and we wait. Another stumbling block we've run into is dealing with strangers in cars pulling over and talking to the kids. The dilemma with autism is you're constantly teaching socialization. So it's very hard to turn around and say don't talk to this particular person. Teaching to discern between good and bad strangers has been a big challenge.

We also teach Chris how to cross with traffic lights – when to go, when to stop. I've often thought how valuable it would be to build a working model of a sidewalk and a street with a crosswalk and lights for persons with disabilities. There is so much talk about building a resource center for autism. This would be perfect to include, since it's such an important thing. Have the department of transportation put up a stop sign and traffic light, and then have the instructors drive a car and teach the children traffic safety. You can pay back the community by inviting the blind, deaf, and Down's syndrome children to utilize it. There's nothing better than a working model.

It's very important to remember when teaching anything to a child with autism, but especially traffic safety, that you generalize the lesson. Not only does your child have to learn to stop at the street corner you're teaching, but she must also learn to stop at any street where there's the slightest possibility of traffic. Every chance you get, consistently emphasize the lesson, and have everyone else with your child reinforce it as well, (siblings, therapists, and grandparents).

A typical child will understand to stop and look before crossing any street because she understands that cars are cars; not so a child who has autism. A child with autism might say to herself, "Okay, when I cross this street I was taught that I have to stop and look." At the next street she may walk right across without looking because she wasn't taught to generalize. It's very important to be very consistent with the traffic scenario every time, every street, everywhere there's the possibility of traffic. "Stop and look." But you must also transfer the concept to other moving vehicles as well. If not careful, kids with autism can get in their minds that they only stop for cars. "That's not a car. It's a big bus so I'm going to cross."

Social awareness and safety when shopping

We spend a lot of time working on social awareness and safety when shopping in the mall. The mall is a good location because it's an easy place to learn socialization. There's parking, traffic. We eat, wait on line, use the public bathroom, and shop there. It's vast and there's even security there. The mall's a great lesson plan.

When we're in the mall, we give Chris the opportunity to tell us where he'd like to go and let him lead us. We utilize the time to train him to be on his own. If he says "Suncoast Video" we say, "Okay. Just stay close to us," and we walk behind him and watch how he interacts with people. Does he get off course? Does he notice people in his path? We let him take different routes to different stores and we teach him to say "Excuse me" if he bumps into someone.

Once in the store a number of things need to be taught. The first thing I always do, however, is go up to the staff and introduce them to my son if possible. I especially make this a habit in small, local stores that we frequent regularly. This way I let them know Chris has autism and what that means they can expect. In a video store, for instance, I tell them that because of the disorder they may see him rearrange some of the movies, carry a few movies around, and get a little anxious on line. I let them know that they may have to instruct him to put the movie on the counter a number of times. Oh, and I always add, "By the way, if my son happens to tear or break something, please let us know. We will be more than happy to pay for it. We're not allowing him to do this, but it is such an urge sometimes that it may happen." I'm clueing them in right away that, yes, he has a disorder and there are some things they might have to deal with. However, that doesn't mean he's going to run rampant in the store.

There are times and places, of course, when you won't be able to introduce yourself and get staff to know you, so you have to teach your child there are simply things you cannot do. It is not okay to push people out of the way, pick something up and leave the store, rearrange things, or wander into Employee Only or No Exit doorways. These are rules the child must follow in stores, but also in other places too, otherwise he's going to get in trouble. The way you behave in stores carries over everywhere. The experience of the store is not only a safety experience, but a social experience as well.

Check-out time is an excellent teaching experience because the child has to be taught how to stand on line – this is a tremendous issue. The first time we stood on line Chris's legs were shaking. So we'd keep telling him, "Okay, one more minute. You're doing a great job. Tomorrow you can come back and get another movie. Soon it'll be Chris's turn. Okay. You're next." He actually stood on line and waited his turn! It was a great experience. Some kids with autism simply can't wait like that, however; that's the time you have to explain your situation to the store owner and ask him to serve you first.

Once at the counter, we taught Chris how to conduct the transaction. Counter experience is tremendous because he's being spoken to by a merchant and has to follow directions. First he has to learn to place the item down. I then tell him to buy it and give him money. We're even starting to teach him what the coins and bills mean. Right now he simply hands over the money and doesn't even care about the change. All he wants is his merchandise. In time and with repetition, though, he will learn. Another thing Chris had to learn was that he couldn't open things merely because he wanted them. He understood early on that when he opened something he ended up getting it. So we had to counteract that lesson with one which taught him that opening things was not permissible.

Kids with autism tend to mark things as their territory; Chris used to mark with spit. Obviously he had to learn he couldn't do this. So day after day we'd say, "Okay, stop. If you want to buy that you can't spit. Hold it and then we're going to go up to the counter. Are you ready to pay?"

"Pay" was a big thing. It meant you are ready to go on that line and get what you want. So he'd choose something and show me.

"Is that the one you want?"

"Yes."

"How many movies?"

"One movie."

"Okay. Wait to pay."

Eventually Chris learned and now he comes to me and says "pay" when he's ready.

We also use shopping as a language experience by encouraging Chris to tell us what he wants to purchase. Or if a little boy comes in and stands next to him we might tell him to say "Hi". "Chris, that boy likes Barney too. Show him the Barney movie." It's really another opportunity to help teach socialization. Safety training while shopping easily generalizes into social and everyday life training. Your child is learning how to fit into the mainstream.

Chris is always encouraged to talk to people, follow rules, and motor plan. If you as a parent are thinking all the time and utilize that time to teach your child, shopping can be a tremendous tool for safety and socialization. Everything can come into play. Is it tedious to teach? No. I'm not making it a school lesson. Going to the mall with Chris has taught me that there's not one opportunity you can't utilize to work with your child, and it seems to carry over into everything. The mall's become a great lesson plan.

No matter what safety lesson you are teaching your child there is always one hard and fast rule I live by. I try to see myself as Chris. I become him and say to myself, "If this was coming at me in this way, I'd feel like this." I try to picture how he would feel in situations. We even have our therapists do it sometimes.

In order to be clear about training you really have to spell things out. Talk in a way that your child will understand. My son and other children with autism are different in the way they perceive things. You've got to try to explain situations from their angle. Remember, it takes repetition, clear concise speaking, and short direct commands. Slip into that autistic suit to see why you might be failing in communication.

What to do when lost

You can set up marvelous life lessons at the mall. We are about to begin showing Chris where to go if he is lost and what being lost means. On a daily basis we will break the concept down explaining why he would need to go to the security office, and also why he would need to dial 911. (Understand that the ultimate end of the lesson could take a year.)

It's important that Chris realize he can get help if we're ever separated. Although we keep very close to Chris at all times the possibility still exists that he could run or get separated in a crowd. Maybe he'll need help because he's confused or sees an emergency. What if I faint or have a heart attack? He needs to know how to show his ID and shoe tag in an emergency. I hope whoever finds me will also see my card identifying Chris as being autistic, and that they will look for him if he has wandered off. After understanding the reasons he would need to get help, we will show Chris where the security office is and what he has to do there. Throughout the teaching we're going also to have to explain who not to go to for help. He has to understand that some people may take advantage of him.

Next what we will do is put the lesson into action by utilizing five people and stationing ourselves throughout the mall. The security office will also participate. Chris will be given the following instructions. "Okay, Chris, Mommy and Daddy are going to stay here. Your job is to go to the security office and tell them you need help." Everyone stationed around the mall will watch and see if he goes to the security office. Once he reaches the security office the guard will ask, "Can I help you?"

"Help, please."

"Oh, you need help." Chris should then show him his ID.

"Oh, your name is Chris Davis. Okay. I'll call your parents. Come inside."

This lesson will take at least a few months to do successfully. Then we have to keep reminding him of everything he learned over and over again. But if I do it well enough and generalize and talk about it enough, he will eventually be able to say to himself, "I'm lost or I don't know what to do now so I have to find somebody." Out of these simple safety lessons at the mall come many complicated lessons that can be learned. Let's say Chris is approached one day and someone makes some wise guy remark to him. If he knows a situation is escalating or he feels afraid, then he knows he can also go to someone for help.

In addition to teaching about security guards and the security office we also believe it is very important to teach your child several meeting places in case you are separated at the mall. Sometimes you may teach about security and the security office, but your teaching might fly out the window if there's a real stressful situation. These kids could just lose everything they were taught. It's especially good to teach them locations that they like. We've started teaching Chris that if he gets separated he can go to the video store because while he may forget the route to the security office, he will always remember the route to the video store. It's implanted in his mind because he loves it so much. No matter where we enter the mall he always knows how to get to the video store.

It's also very important to teach that people they know can be just as helpful as security guards or police officers. In other words, the friendly store clerk in Hollywood Video can help him, the neighbor who says "Hello" can help him, and his sister's friends can help him. Give your child a variety of people as resources. Remember, these children have weak self-help skills. It doesn't occur to them that the neighbor they see every day can help them. A lot of people teach that police, firefighters, and security officers can help, but it's important to point out other people who can also help. This way you're generalizing the idea that there are other people besides Daddy to ask for help. This seems very trivial, but it's actually most important that these children understand they can go through life and ask other people for help without having to go to the police. After all, going to the police can escalate small situations needlessly.

One of the basics of teaching safety is self-preservation. You have to instill great self-worth so your child likes herself and realizes she is worth being safe. If I can teach my son self-worth then I can go on to show him that there are things which cannot happen to him because he's a valuable human being. So if somebody makes fun of him, pushes him, steals from him, or knocks him down he will know that is not acceptable. It's against him and he is valuable and cannot let that happen. It is a crime and he needs to report it – "You stand up for yourself." You need to teach your child that he or she is a valuable person and this cannot be done to them.

Entrance and exits

The first time I took Chris to a department store to shop for movies we went up the escalator. I pointed out landmarks to him as we walked through the store so he'd get familiar with his sur-roundings. Then we went down the escalator to leave. Next time we went to the store he took the right route, but staring him in the face was the down escalator. He was very confused because he knew he was supposed to ride it up, but something didn't feel quite right. As he started to go, I stopped him and he became upset because he thought I was trying to keep him from going upstairs. He didn't understand it was the wrong escalator; so began my up/down teaching on the escalator.

We'd been in department stores before with escalators where we taught him how to get on – put your foot down, now you stay, hold on. Then getting off he also had to be taught to pay attention and not wander. "We're coming to the end. You've got to look. Look. Now keep moving once you get off. You can't stop." So we did go over escalator safety, but we never went over up and down.

It was important to teach Chris to recognize the words for up and down because he has visual spatial problems and doesn't always see things clearly. So I took him and said, "Let me show you." Then I pointed down and showed him the word. We went over this a number of times and then I did the same with up.

"What's that say?"

"Down."

"Down. Where do you want to go?"

"Up."

"Up. Okay. Let's look for the up escalator."

Now when Chris is confronted with an escalator he looks for the sign, recognizes the words up and down and understands the difference, gets on carefully, gets off, and follows the route.

Chris was next taught to generalize the concepts and understand there are a number of ways to go up and down. You can go down the stairs or take the elevator down as well. Another lesson was to learn how to ride elevators. Chris had to learn how to read the floor and identify it, press the button, get on safely, get out and get back in. It was also necessary for him to learn how to get out politely and say "Excuse me."

"Where do you want to go?"

"Toys."

"Where are toys?"

"Three."

"Three. Okay, let's go over. You have to press this button to get on the elevator. How do you get on the elevator? What if there are people on the elevator? Now we have to press '3' right away. You have to look up here, and when '3' comes on you have to get off."

Remember that mall entrances have automatic doors for disabled people. One of Chris's first lessons was that you don't push the button. We had to cover the fact that people are coming in, that it's their turn and you move away. In my opinion, learning manners is an important part of safety. We also had to do the same type of teaching with doors and the concepts of "push" and "pull." Chris had to understand that you wait for people to come out before you enter, and that sometimes doors swing and you have to wait and be careful. We made him aware of automatic doors and taught him to step on the mat to make them open. We even went through a couple of revolving doors so he wouldn't be nervous about them. First I demonstrated, then we just stood in the revolving door and left it open enough so we could back out.

Bathrooms

Using a public bathroom requires a number of safety and social awareness issues. First Chris had to learn to wait to pull his pants down until he got into the bathroom stall. A lot of times he would pull his pants down in the middle of a restaurant if we asked him if he had to "go potty" because being naked to him was not a bad thing. Chris didn't realize that public nudity is a problem, so I taught him to keep his pants on until he goes into the bathroom. "No, let's wait. We pull our pants down when we get in the stall."

The basis of safety training is that you have to be aware of your surroundings. You can't just wander in and pull down your pants and pee without caring who's around. It's not in your make-up to care, but it's my job to teach you to care. In order to survive there are some things you're going to have to learn about life.

Next I trained Chris to go into the stall and lock the door. "Close the door so it's private." I use the word "private" because I've used it enough so that I think he knows what it means. "This is a private thing you do." Then I taught Chris to clean up and flush. I believe it is very important to teach him that when going to the bathroom there are a lot of things about cleanliness and privacy to understand. He can't just touch everything. I have to teach him about sanitation. In other words my bathroom is clean, but a public bathroom is not. It doesn't occur to him that a bathroom seat is dirty, for instance, and he shouldn't touch it. I try to emphasize never to touch anything around him because it's dirty. You don't play with the seat or put your hands in the water. You don't pick up paper. When we're finished we wash our hands at the sink because we're clean, and then we leave.

We speak a lot about privacy. Going to the bathroom is a private thing; no one should be looking at you. Therefore you don't pull down your pants in the middle of the bathroom. In fact, the first thing I taught Chris was that we don't pull our pants down till we're right next to the toilet. Manners are important so you wait your turn to use a stall. Once in the stall you always close the door before you pull your pants down. Before you leave you pull your pants up and make sure you're dressed.

I try to emphasize to Chris never to linger in the bathroom when someone is talking to him. These things are obvious to us, but not to our kids. Much of this I try to teach by example so he will model my behavior. I make a point of being very matter-of-fact in the bathroom. "Let's do our business here, finish, and get out. We don't socialize." I show with my body language that I'm keeping private.

Locker rooms and swimming

Chris and I frequently go swimming and in order to do so we change in a locker room. We're around people who are dressing and taking showers so this is a whole new set of social lessons for him to learn. As in the public bathrooms, I teach a lot through modeling and instruction. I show Chris not to invade other people's space while they're standing next to him getting dressed. "Okay, Chris. Let's put on our bathing suits and let's go." I teach him not to stop and stare and not to look at people in the shower. Showers are private. I also have to teach him that we don't linger naked – this isn't home. You get dressed right away or you cover yourself.

Here again Chris has to learn hygiene awareness. The floor is dirty so we wear shoes and don't walk in our bare feet. I also teach him that we have a locker, a private place where we keep our things and that other people have their private lockers. We don't touch theirs and nobody touches ours. There are some big lessons to learn in the locker room – being safe within your space, privacy, staring, wandering over to someone who's using the urinal to look, bathroom cleanliness, putting your clothes away, knowing where to come back and get your clothes, and exiting.

When it comes to actually swimming, it has to be emphasized that when you teach pool safety you must generalize it to show that the same safety rules apply for a lake, a river, or even a bathtub. As in everything, you must generalize whatever it is you're teaching whether you do it through pictures or visits to actual locations. Children with autism are attracted to water. If you don't generalize the concept of water safety in a pool the rules are not the same to them for a lake. In their minds the rules are only for the pool. So you have to show them all bodies of water and that these safety precautions apply everywhere.

Restaurants

At the restaurant I concentrate on a couple of safety and social awareness issues. First Chris must learn that he has to wait to get a table; he can't just go in and sit anywhere he wants. We tell him we know it's hard, but soon it will be his turn. I always let the restaurant know about his disorder and explain that he will be eating a lot of food brought from home because he has a special diet. Informing the staff about my son is also for safety, so that if anything happens, they are aware of the problem. For instance, Chris stims a lot and flaps his hands when he's excited and happy. I won't stop those behaviors unless they're harmful, but to others around us his actions could cause concern.

Chris does sometimes want to get out of the booth and walk back and forth. If he really can't sit there any more and we're not finished eating, we'll let him get up. That means he has a lot to learn. Here comes a waitress, for example, with a full tray and Chris is taking a walk reading his book totally unaware of her. It won't occur to him that he has to get out of the way. It's important for us to teach him about people carrying things, hot things, other people's private things, dirty things, and even things on the floor. Not long ago, Chris used to pick up everything he saw and taste it. Frequenting restaurants also helps reinforce socialization: there's a time to go, to leave, and to pay. You can't wander and go up to another table because you see something you want. And he learns to communicate by ordering. "What do you want? Tell the waitress."

Be sure to bring things to the restaurant that your child likes. You want to have something that will distract from an upsetting event. How about coloring books? Then if your child needs to be by herself and settle down, she can color quietly. Otherwise you may get a monstrous explosion in the restaurant where the child's jumping out of the booth, throwing things, and hitting herself because she has nothing to occupy herself.

Travel

When traveling the first thing I do is tell the front desk my son has autism when I make the telephone reservation. I explain what they might see in the lobby and that they shouldn't be concerned. A late check-out might be needed, I explain, because we may not be able to get him ready. When we arrive at the hotel I go over this information again. I might also ask for specific necessities for Chris to make him comfortable. "Can you tell me if there are stores around that make fresh bread and can you get it to me because it's really important to his diet?" I've got to teach the hotel staff that his needs, as trivial as they may appear, are just as important as the ramp for a person in a wheelchair. To my son, having the correct bread roll is crucial.

One of the big issues for your child with hotels may be understanding that you will return to your home. We teach Chris a social story to prepare him: "We are a family going in a car. We are going to Washington, DC. There we will look at stores and we will stay for two days. Then we will come back home and we will be happy." We always show him that we are going somewhere for a purpose and it is happy. We are going to stay in a room, but we are coming back.

We also use a calendar to show when we will arrive and when we will leave. Then we count the days and go over it with Chris. Each day we do the calendar and count the number of days left before we go home; in this way he knows what's expected of him. Otherwise Chris may not understand that he is not staying in the hotel forever. It's very important to give him a timeframe so he knows there's an ending to what's happening. Another thing we're sure to do is bring things Chris likes and uses at home; things that make him comfortable, like books and pillows. We think through his whole day so he has what's important to him at all times.

Obviously, hotels are unfamiliar living quarters so there are safety issues that need to be taken into consideration. We immediately go over the hotel room ourselves. Are there windows that can be opened? How high up are we? What kind of locks are on the doors? Anything in the bathroom we're not familiar with like switches, heaters or coffee machines we explain to Chris. He is told exactly what he may or may not touch in the room. A lot of kids are hiders so I would make sure they know they're not supposed to go into closets or other small spaces. Be sure to keep in-between rooms locked.

Chris needs to understand that the hotel is a strict environment. We repeatedly stress that he is not to open the door: "We don't go out until Mommy and Daddy go out. You cannot wander." If we know we're going to visit a specific destination like the zoo or museum we try to introduce it in a social story so that Chris is prepared. When we leave the hotel room we go over the route, the number of the room, and the number of the floor just in case Chris wanders off. The lobby is another off-limits place unless he's with us. We're in a strange situation so we hold hands any time we go anywhere. The bottom line is that when he's not in his own home he must stay closer to his parents than he normally would. Here are a few safety rules we adhere to when staying at a hotel:

- Make sure Chris has things he's comfortable with
- Make sure Chris knows where he's going
- Make sure Chris knows he will be going home
- Make sure people in the hotel are aware of Chris
- Make sure we're in the quiet part of the hotel
- Make sure Chris understands this is not a time for exploration.

Movie theaters

Although attending movie theaters was more a social than a safety issue, going to them was still a tough challenge. We explained to Chris what he would see ahead of time, but when we walked into the lobby it was very confusing and he did not want to go in. There were noise, lines, smell, popcorn, people, dirt, hustle and bustle. Our first visit did not work out and we had to leave.

During our next attempt at going to a movie theater we stayed outside until the last minute. We still ran into an unexpected problem, though – the seats. Movie seats spring up if you don't put weight down on them, and Chris was so upset and nervous that I had to keep my hand on his seat the whole time. Throughout the entire movie he was waiting for the seat to spring up. He didn't understand that when he sat down, his weight would hold the seat down. Every time Chris moved even the slightest bit he would feel the seat give and be afraid. We've gone to the theater several times since then, but it's not the easiest of circumstances.

A special note on handling public crisis situations

The tragic events of September 11, 2001 have unfortunately pointed out that even kids with autism can be affected by public crises. The simple truth is that tragedies occur, whether from terrorism, tornado, or fire, but what's learned from one tragedy should be generalized to others. First, children with autism should not be discounted in these situations. Even though they may not quite understand what's going on, they understand the emotions. Some people said their teenagers had experienced rage after September 11; kids who were older were perseverating on ideas like, "I can never go in a plane. All planes crash into the World Trade Center." Kids with autism may be playing in a corner while you have the news on all day, and maybe they don't quite understand it, but they definitely feel the fear, anxiety, and terror.

Be aware that some children with autism actually try to mimic events and emotions that they see over and over again. Children with a lot of language may find it hard to get off the subject: "I can't get on a plane. Bombs are on planes. Bombs are on all planes. I can't go on a plane." You might have to steer them gently away and explain that this is something that happened elsewhere: "You are safe. You are home and not near it. This does not happen every time you get on a plane." Don't overexpose children to the news and talking about events. Turn the TV off to prevent that feeling of fear and sadness. Do, however, talk honestly about the events when your child asks about them and reassure him or her that they are safe.

Let's say your child is exhibiting a lot of disturbance from an event, perhaps having a lot of nightmares. You can encourage her to draw a picture – maybe of the event – and then you can discuss it. Talk a lot; explain things and redirect. If your child is constantly talking about a plane crash, redirect them to another topic or play a movie they like.

Teach your children to take deep breaths if they're nervous. Let them know that their fears are valid. People do have fear and it's not silly or stupid. Let them know that you're afraid too and that their fears are not unfounded. We have to talk about them and address them. Ask your child what they know so you get an idea of what they're thinking. They may have to act out their thoughts or use pictures. Ask if they have questions. Gently explain over and over again so you get the answers into their heads. Use social stories to show what has happened and that they're safe. Use the things you normally use to make your child comfortable. It's okay to say you don't know when asked a question. Don't be ashamed to say you don't know or that you're afraid too. Tell the truth, but tell it gently. Constantly ask what they're thinking and feeling.

We know as adults that you don't have to be involved in a tragedy to be affected by it. Neither do children with autism. A typical child might come to you and tell you that he is scared, but you may only detect by symptomatic behavior that a child with autism has been affected. Young children might be startled by loud noises or have trouble sleeping. Symptoms might be as little as being extra fussy or as severe as having terrible stomach aches. Older children may express fear about their parents' safety. They may exhibit eating disorders, sleep disturbances, anger, or may even focus on retaliation or death. Look for these things and reassure your child that he or she is safe. For older children, especially, emphasize that in time things will return to normal.

Giving our children with autism the training they need to be safe and aware is a tough, full-time job, but a necessary one. No matter what you do, there is one piece of advice that should always hold true: look at your kid *as* a kid. Be intuitive and put yourself in their place. Learn how it feels to be them. I always try to see myself as Chris. In my mind I become him and say to myself, "If this is coming at me in this way, I'd feel like this." I try to picture how he would feel in situations. At times we even do this exercise with our therapists.

What makes kids with autism unsafe is that they are so overwhelmed by externals that they explode. That's why it's very important to know your child and to what he can be exposed. How far can he go on the outside without exploding? The minute you put these kids in situations they can't handle things are going to become very unsafe. They have to be able to handle these overloads, but we also need to know when to back off and not force them into overwhelming situations.

You can't expect everybody to tiptoe around your child. People often don't respect or understand autism. They don't understand that a child with autism cannot express himself and needs a quiet place. Yes, we have to teach people around us about the disorder if we want to keep our children safe, but safety is a two-prong issue. Running after our kids all the time to keep them safe is not an option. We also need to give them the tools they need to express themselves and keep themselves safe and aware. I have to teach my son that his feelings are legitimate, and if he can't stand to be touched, for example, that's okay.

In order to be clear in safety training you really have to spell things out. Talk in a way that your child is going to understand. Chris is different in the way he perceives things so I've got to try to explain things from his angle. You can't teach safety and awareness as you would with a typical child. It may take three months to teach Chris to move away when someone is walking by with a tray of food.

Slip into that autistic suit to see why you might be failing in communication. You have constantly to teach the same way ABA is conducted: reward good behaviors, ignore bad behaviors. It takes repetition, clear concise speaking, and short direct commands. We constantly reinforce what Chris learns by rewarding and praising when he does something right.

It is important to remember that safety and awareness training is a very broad issue because it is also tied to living in the community as fully as possible. Our job becomes teaching, showing what we expect of our children, and then generalizing that knowledge so it becomes a way of life. There are going to be kids who can never handle going to the mall by themselves, and there are going to be kids who get their own apartment, shop, and work. But whatever your child's potential, the important thing is for them to get along in the world.

A guy with autism told me at a lecture I gave that he gets extremely nervous if he's in a long line or pulled over in his car. He is so uptight that he gets the immediate fight or flight reaction. "I want to run out of the car and run away. I'm trying to make myself stay there, and I'm twitching and I can't talk. They're looking at me like I'm nuts or I did something wrong. It's the most horrible feeling in the world." He knows intellectually he should stay there and relax, but he can't. He needs to be able to say that he has autism and the people around him need to understand the disorder.

What's misunderstood about the disorder more than anything is this type of situation, and this is what causes the misinterpretations and misunderstandings and safety issues. When I won the "End The Victims' Silence" Advocacy Award it was stressed that people with autism are the perfect victims. They often can't speak or express themselves well. They act in a weird manner so why believe them?

To get along in the world successfully, people with autism need to be aware of themselves and have pride in who they are. My son joins in the community of people, but he's still allowed to be himself. I'm always reinforcing his participation at the restaurant table, for instance, without suppressing any harmless behaviors. We get stares, but I am constantly telling Chris that even though people turn around I am proud of him. A sense of self-worth and the desire to take care of yourself is essential to participate in the community safely and happily.

Epilogue

I urge all parents, educators, police officers and politicians to take a fresh, unbiased look at our children. Utilize their strengths and do not capitalize on their differences. Allow them their dreams and do not exclude them from everyday life. Recognize their heroic struggle, befriend them and help them create a place of comfort and love.

As I am writing this, Chris is trying on a pair of orange tinted sunglasses. He is looking in the mirror, smiling, twisting his body, joking around. I am laughing, telling him how funny he is. Now I am holding him tight. My son has taught me so much. I do not speak for him because he has nothing to say but because many do not make the effort to listen. I do not clench my fists because he is weak but because many will take advantage of him. I do not keep him close to me because of pity but because of love. I am richer for loving him.

My boy is so strong, so creative. Chris has many sensory issues and has always been sensitive to people eating in front of him. The smell, the food and especially the noise of chewing, all disturb him. He will give me dirty looks if I chew my food loudly. I have learned to eat quietly around him. The other day Chris handed me a piece of doughnut and motioned to me to eat it. I thanked him and proceeded to chew and swallow softly. Chris quickly shook his head "no" and made a loud chewing noise. He wanted me to eat my food vigorously – to imitate the loud noise.

When I did, he looked away, tightened his body and clenched his fists. He then pointed for me to do it again and again; each time his face would contort and he would shake a little but demand that I eat loudly over and over again. Chris was desensitizing himself; in fact he created his own eating program! What strength, intelligence, and creativity he has. We can now all eat comfortably around him.

My son is a solid, viable, loving human being. Respect his right to be different and admire his tenacity. You might become richer for it, too.

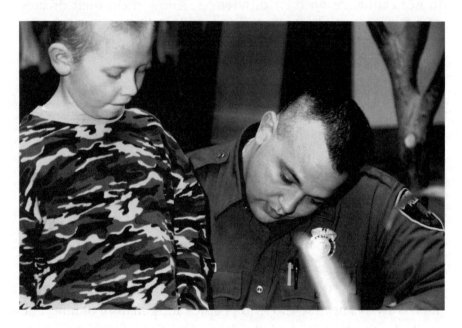

Emergency Alert Window Decals Sheet

Autism Information Card

Front

AUTISM

COMMUNICATION

May be non-verbal or have limited verbal abilities. **May** appear deaf,may not respond to verbal cues.**May** repeat words or phrases in place of normal communications.**May** have difficulty expressing needs, uses gestures or Points.

BEHAVIOR

May have tantrums-display extreme distress for no apparent reason. **May** exhibit inappropriate laughing or giggling. **May** show no real fear of dangers. **May** have little or no eye contact. **May** appear insensitive to pain. **May** be sensitive to touch, sound or bright lights. **May** exhibit self-stimulating behaviors: Hand flapping, finger flicking, body rocking.

IN CRIMINAL JUSTICE SITUATIONS

May not understand rights. **May** have difficulty remembering facts or details of offenses. **May** become anxious in new situations. **May** not understand consequences of their actions.

Back

AUTISM

HELPFUL HINTS FOR INTERACTIONS WITH INDIVIDUALS WITH AUTISM

- Use simple language; speak slowly and clearly.
- Use concrete terms and ideas.
- Repeat simple questions; allowing time (10-15 seconds) for a response.
- Proceed slowly and give praise and encouragement.
- Do not attempt to physically stop self-stimulating behavior.

REMEMBER: Each individual with autism is unique and may act or react differently. PLEASE contact a responsible person who is familiar with the individual.

For more information, call 800-3**AUTISM**.

Appendix B

Emergency ID Card Instruction

It is very important that you always have an issue date on the ID card, especially if the photograph is not current. You wouldn't want workers at an emergency worried that someone might be missing because the ID card is outdated and your child looks nothing like her picture. Here are the steps to make your child's ID card:

1. Scan a recent picture of your child.

2. Crop the picture to 1½" by 2" (I find this size to be the clearest).

3. Print out the picture.

4. Open any design or layout program with which you can make postcards or business cards.

5. Click on "business cards."

6. Start from the "scratch" section.

7. Choose your size and layout (how many images you want on a page and how big you want them).

8. Click on "graphics" and select any picture. Crop it to the same size as your child's photo (in this case I used "Abe").

9. Once your photo is in place, add two text boxes. Put one box underneath the photo and one to its side.

10. Under the photo type your child's name and that she is autistic. In my case I "wrote nonverbal autistic child". Also type in the issue date of your card.

11. In the box next to the photo type all vital information that police or emergency personnel would need about your child if you were unconscious or unable to speak.

12. Type in: "CALL CONTACTS IMMEDIATELY!"

13. Print out your page.

14. Place your child's picture on to one of the cards in place of "Abe."

15. Cut out and laminate the card (this leaves me several cards on which to update photos of my child throughout the year).

16. Attach the photo ID card of your child to the back of your driver's license with a piece of tape.

17. If you prefer to keep the ID with your keys, punch a hole in the card and insert your key ring.

Here is some of the information you may wish to include on your ID card:

- Name
- Hair and eye color

- Height and weight
- Visible birth marks
- Age
- Address
- Issue date
- Contact numbers
- Allergies to food and medication.

Be sure your contact numbers are current and identify the person's relationship (parent, caretaker) to the child. Information about allergies is useful in case someone offers your child a soda or candy to calm them. You might also want to add the name your child answers to and how she reacts when afraid or upset. Try to be as brief as possible.

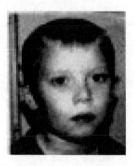

Christopher Helton Davis
Non-Verbal Child w/Autism
Issue Date: 10/10/00

In case of emergency contact:
Bill or Jae Davis (parents)
Hm: 717-555-1212 Wk: 717-555-1212
Birthdate: 12/24/95 sex: male
Height: 4'1" weight: 72lbs
eyes: blue hair: blonde
Address: 123 Oak Rd.
Lancaster, PA.
Child responds to Chris or Chrisy.
Child does not respond to language –
uses a picture communication book
He may avoid eye contact, wave
hands, repeat what you are saying.
He sings when he is afraid or utters
various sounds. He may show no
signs of pain or fear. He may try to
run or avoid being touched. Please
call contact person(s) immediately.

Appendix C

How to Make a Travel Communications Safety Book

1. Get a folder or small notebook.

2. Create a list of personal questions that might be relevant to your child during an emergency. Here are some examples:

    • What's your name?

    • Where do you live?

    • What's your phone number?

    • How old are you?

    • Who's your mother?

    • Who's your father?

    • Who's your sister, brother, grandmother, etc.?

    • What do you like to drink?

    • What do you like to eat?

    • Where do you go to school?

    • What grade are you in?

- What do you like to play with?
- How are you?
- How do you feel?
- Are you hurt?

3.   Print the questions on 2" by 2" square pieces of paper. Keep the background color the same for all questions. Insert 2" by 2" grid.

4.   Illustrate each question with a simple picture: e.g., use a telephone for the question "What's your phone number?" If you prefer, you can use the Mayer-Johnson Communications Symbol Book rather than make your own pictures, but it's nice to personalize the safety book if you can.

5.   Take another background color and write the answers to each of the questions. When designing the answers you should try to use the same visual cues used on the question cards. It's also good to use photos of the actual places referred to in the questions. Put in illustrations of question and answer cards.

6.   Attach small squares of Velcro to the back of each question and answer card. Then attach Velcro to the folder or notebook pages. Place all questions on one page and all answers on the opposite page. Size your pictures so they can all fit on one open page. (You don't want to thumb through different pages to find an answer.) Make a few double-sided Velcro strips that will attach both to the notebook and to the picture cards. The strips should be long enough to hold both the question and answer at the same time.

7. Make a cover that clearly says Travel Communication and Safety Book so people will know to use it in an emergency.

Now you need to teach your child how to answer the questions. Begin by having him match one picture to its answer by using the visual cues. Hand the question directly to your child attached to the sentence strip with room for him to place the answer. Continue until he can discriminate between each picture. Don't forget to verbalize the question and answer each time. This book is a vital tool in keeping your child calm in an emergency situation and in helping emergency personnel to gather important information.

You can also help your child remain calm in the car by letting him know where you are going in order to prepare him. One way to communicate your destination is by attaching Velcro to your visor or dashboard. Then take photographs of traveled places frequently visited by your family. Label the photographs and attach Velcro to the back of each one. Always attach your next destination to the visor and announce it to your child. You can even place a series of photographs showing the entire route you'll be taking. Before long your child may be telling you where he wants to go by picking out which photo he wants displayed.

(Sample) Travel and Safety Communication Car Book

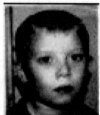

My name is...

What's your name?

Chris Davis

Who is your dad?

My dad is Bill Davis.

Who is your mom?

My mom is Jae Davis.

(Sample) Travel and Safety Communication Car Book

Where do you live?   My address is...

What is your phone number?   My phone number is 555-1212

How old are you?   I am seven years old.

7

(Sample) Travel and Safety Communication Car Book

Where do you go to school?

I go to school in Baltimore

How are you?   I'm fine.   I am sick.

Who is your sister?   My sister is Jessica Davis.

(Sample) Travel and Safety Communication Car Book

Who is your grandma?

My grandma is Hilda Davis.

What do you like to eat?

I like to eat peanut butter sandwiches and doughnuts

What do you like to drink?

I like to drink pepsi.

(Sample) Travel and Safety Communication Car Book

Are you hurt?   no   yes

I need to go.   I am tired.   Ask me a yes/no question

I am hungry   I am thirsty   I am cold.

Appendix D

Safety Social Stories

When I am Hurt in an Accident

Some times children get hurt in car accidents.

Emergency Responders are called to help.

E.M.S   Police   Firefighters

When Chris is hurt in a car accident Chris will lay still, resting, until someone comes to help him.

Emergency Responders will come in an ambulance with a loud siren and flashing red lights.

It will be a man or a woman. She or he will talk quietly to Chris.

They may ask Chris some questions.

They may ask Chris where it hurts, or to move his fingers and toes.

 They may ask Chris if he can hear them, or if he understands.

They may ask Chris to keep his eyes open and to try and stay awake.

Chris will answer yes or no, or point to the body parts that hurt.

They will put Chris on a little white board and put straps around him.

This keeps Chris from falling off when they carry him to the ambulance.

Chris will try not to move.

 They will drive Chris to the hospital.

 At the hospital doctors and nurses will help Chris.

 Doctors and nurses will make Chris feel better.

When Chris wakes up Mom, Dad and Jessi will be beside him.

Smiling

What I do when I Hear the Fire Alarm in my Home

Usually, there is not a real fire. I have to practice with my family just in case.

 When I hear a fire alarm, I stop what I am doing and carefully do the steps in the drill I have been practicing with my family.

If I am in bed in my room, first I get out of bed and down onto the floor. Second, I crawl towards the door. I crawl so I don't breathe in the smoke from the fire.

 I crawl to the stairs and sit down and go down the stairs on my butt to the front door.

 When I get to the front door I go outside and wait by the tree in my front yard for the rest of my family. Where I am safe.

 Soon my family will come and the firefighters will put out the fire.

A Fire at Chris's House

One day there was a fire at Chris's house. The fire was burning downstairs and the house was filled with smoke.

 When Chris heard the fire alarm, he could not do what he had practiced with his family. It would not be safe to go towards the fire. So Chris laid on the floor so he would not breathe in the smoke.

Chris laid very still, and hit the floor with his fist over and over again to make noise so the firefighters would know where he was. Chris knew a firefighter would be there soon to take him safely outside to his family.

When Chris saw the firefighter he was scary looking. He looked very big, he had an air tank on his back and a scary gas mask over his face that made his voice sound strange.

Chris remembered that all of the scary things protected the firefighters from the fire and smoke.

The firefighter called to Chris and motioned for Chris to come towards him. Chris went to the firefighter immediately.

The firefighter picked Chris up into his arms. Chris did not fight. Chris closed his eyes and held on real tight so the firefighter could carry him out of the house.

When Chris got outside, someone wrapped him in a blanket. Soon Chris, Mom and Dad and sister were kissing and hugging him. That was the best part!

Riding in the Car

 Sometimes I ride in a car and travel to other places.

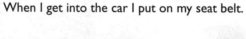 When I get into the car I put on my seat belt.

Sometimes the car stops unexpectedly, a police officer may come to the window to talk to my mom.

I try to wait calmly, I do not get out of the car unless my mom or dad tell me to. I like to watch the flashing red lights

Soon the police officer will give my mom a piece of paper and we will be able to take our ride again.

Meeting Officer Chris

Today Chris is meeting a police officer.

Chris is going to the Mall.

To Suncoast Video.

We will sit and open movies.

Chris will meet a policeman.
His name is Chris too.

Chris will shake hands with the policeman.

Chris will wear a police hat.

Chris will take pictures with the policeman.

After that Chris will go to Boscov's.

Chris will buy a movie or CD.

Then Chris and Mom and Dad will go and eat pizza and soda.

Then we will go home.

Going to the Autism Rally in D.C.

Chris and his family are going on vacation.

 We are driving to Washington D.C. to stay at a hotel.

 We will leave early in the morning, it will look like night outside.

   Chris and Jessi will sleep in the car on the way.

When Chris wakes up, we will be at the hotel.

 At the hotel Chris will swim and watch videos.

Daddy and Jessi will go to the rally for a little while.

 Chris and Mom will drive to the new mall.

  After the mall we will go to the hotel to watch videos Chris bought.

To stay safe Chris will not go out of the room without mom or dad.

Chris will not open the hotel room door unless mom or dad tell him to.

Chris will not go into the elevator without mom or dad.

Chris will memorize his room
number in case he gets lost.

ROOM #

Soon everyone will be tired and go to
sleep at the hotel.

In the morning when Chris
wakes up, Chris will eat and
swim and watch his videos.

Mom will pack and get ready for the ride
home.

Chris, mom, dad and Jessi will be
home soon.

Index

ABA (applied behavior analysis) 107
accident, when I am hurt in (safety social stories) 157–9
aggression/aggressive behavior 14, 34–5
handling 68–9
alarms and screen doors, install 97–8
allergies to food and/or drugs 77, 81
altercations, involvement in 42–3
calling law enforcement because of 46
ambulance and emergency room workers, challenges for 75–81
evaluating for injury 76–7
overview 80–1
Americans with Disabilities Act 21
animals
fear of 32, 38
protective responses to 62
removing 49
anti-social behaviors, don't get angry at 56–7
approaching
from behind, avoidance of 62

slowly and calmly 80
argumentative behavior 60
arrest 62
articulation, bad 60
assess for injury 76–7, 80
attachment, inappropriate 29–30, 37
attention of autistic person, catching and focusing 50
autism
characteristics 23–38
overview 34–8
definition and origin of name 13
emergency ID card 98–9
as spectrum disorder 14
what is it? 11–15
Autism Society of America 13, 70, 98, 102, 108, 109
Autism Society of Illinois 98, 109
Autism Society of Kentucky 109
automatic doors for disabled people 128
aversion to touch 26, 35
awareness day, hold an 102–3

banging, head 34, 45
Barnett, Jolyne 80
bathrooms 128–9
behavioral problems 14
bizarre or disruptive behavior 42, 46
calling law enforcement because of 42, 46

don't get angry at anti-social behaviors 56–7
don't interpret as belligerent 52–3
escalated behavior 65–8
belligerence, odd behaviors appearing as 52–3, 60
biting or hitting other children 34, 43
calling law enforcement because of 46
self- 34, 45
bluntly honest, tendency to be 61
body language, inability to understand 60
body rocking 34
Breaking Autism's Barriers: A Father's Story 104–5
butting, head 34

calm, remain 48–9, 80
car (safety social stories)
riding in 163
travel and safety communication book for 152–6
Center for Disease Control and Prevention 14
cerebral palsy 14, 18, 20
challenging circumstances for emergency responders 63–73
overview 72–3
child abuse, suspected, calling law

enforcement because
of 44–5, 46
"Child with Autism" decals
86
choking 35
clarification of questions or
situation, inability to
ask for 60
comfort zone 36
commotion, keep down to
minimum 49
communication 14
alternative means of 62
give your child a form of
100–1
how to communicate
47–59
overview 60–2
tips 61–2
what you may
encounter at the
scene 60–1
lack of 34
travel and safety
communication car
book (safety social
stories) 152–6
understanding different
forms of 53–7
don't expect a lot
of information
or tactfulness
55–6
don't get angry at
anti-social
behaviors 56–7
picture cards 53
communications safety
book 100
how to make 147–9
computers 53, 62

contact person
ask to register with
police 48
call immediately in
emergency 48, 61
covering ears with hands
37, 60
crime
committing without
understanding they've
done something
wrong 46
conscious participation
in? 70–1
victims of 20–1
inability to
understand that
they are 37
crying and laughter,
inappropriate 28, 36
custody, taking into 69–70

danger
lack of sense of 18, 33,
38
dangerous behaviors,
handling 68–9
Davis, Christopher 10,
12–13, 17–18, 21,
23, 25–8, 30–3,
41–3, 47, 49, 51–2,
54–7, 59, 64, 68–9,
71, 89–92, 97, 99,
101–3, 110–12,
115–18, 120–34,
136–40, 152,
157–68
Davis, Hilda 155
Davis, Jae 18, 54, 97, 99,
115–17, 152

Davis, Jessica (Jessi)
154–6, 154, 159
deaf, appearing to be 38
Debbaudt, Dennis vi
delayed responses, allow
for 61
developmental delay 47
developmental disability
20
direct language and short
phrases, using 52, 61
disability training 21
disruptive or bizarre
behavior, calling law
enforcement because
of 42, 46
Down's syndrome 18
autistic 98
dress, inappropriate 45
drug abuse, autistic
behavior resembling
symptoms of 41, 44
calling law enforcement
because of 46
drugs, using autistic
children to deliver 71
Dyna Voxes/Dyna Mites
53

ears, covering with hands
37, 60
eating
disorders 14, 60
inappropriate objects,
e.g. rocks, mud, glass
(pica) 46
echolalia and echoic
behavior 29, 36, 53,
60

educational presentations
107–8
education
for emergency
responders
concerning autism
21–2
and involvement, of
parents 108–9
elevators 127
Emergency Alert Window
Decals Sheet 141
Emergency Medical
Services (EMS) 79,
167
emergency
alert decals 98
approaching autistic
person in case of 47
ID card instruction
143–5
ID tag 99–100
medical technicians 20
responders
challenging
circumstances
for 63–73
how parents can
work together
with 95–113
room
gaining
cooperation in
77–80
workers 20
challenges for
75–81
emotional abuse 21
emotional detachment
(obliviousness to
emotions) 31–2, 37

encounters with autistic
person, preparing for
long 48–53
don't interpret odd
behaviors as
belligerent 52–3
don't make it a contest
64
don't touch or take by
hand 51
keep animals away 49
keep commotion down
49
non-response does not
imply guilt 50
remain calm 48–9
repeat short, direct
phrases 50
use direct language and
avoid idioms 52
use soft gestures 52
"End the Victims' Silence"
Advocacy Award 138
entrances and exits 126–8
escalated behavior 65–8
escalators 126–7
evaluating for injury 76–7
eye contact
avoidance of 35, 60
wait for 61
gouging 34

F & M College 13
face or neck, do not touch
61
facial expressions, inability
to read 37
fear 34
of animals 32

fight or flight behaviors
60, 65, 67
finger moving/play 34, 45
fire
lack of understanding of
38
rescue 83–7
overview 86–7
safety social stories
fire at Chris's
house 161–2
what I do when I
hear the fire
alarm in my
home 160
firefighters 18, 20, 83,
85–7
Fitzgibbons, Mike 79
flapping hands 34, 41, 45

genius 14
Gohier vs City of
Colorado Springs (no.
98–1149) 21
Grandin, Temple 31
guilt, non-response/lack of
eye contact does not
imply 50, 61

Hagelgans, Battalion Chief
Duane 86
hand(s)
don't take autistic person
by 51
flapping 34, 41, 45
keep down 61
Harrisburg, Pennsylvania
11
head
banging 34, 45

butting 34
rocking 34
tapping 34
heat, lack of understanding
of 38
Heim, Chief vi
hitting or biting other
children 34, 43
calling law enforcement
because of 46
hotels 131–3
hyperactivity or extreme
passivity 27–8, 36

ID (identity)
autism emergency ID
card 98–9, 143–5
have your child wear
emergency ID tag
99–100
look for in an emergency
47–8, 61, 80
and safety procedures
110–12
idioms, avoiding 52, 61
ignoring what you say 60
incidental play 107
infantile autism 27–8
information
don't expect a lot of
55–6
obsessive recitations of
53, 61
injuries 35
self- 14
injury
evaluating for 62, 76–7,
80
insensitivity to pain 25, 35

install screen doors and
alarms 97–8

jealousy, immunity to 31
Jimmy 115–16
jokes, inability to
understand 37, 60

Keares, the vi

Lancaster City Bureau of
Fire 86
Lancaster City Bureau of
Police vi, 45
Lancaster General Hospital
80
language disorders 14
laughter and crying,
inappropriate 28, 36
lavatories, public 128–9
law enforcement
overview 45–6
pocket cards 109–10
shoplifting and store
disturbances 89–94
why it may be called
39–46
light(s)
protective responses to
62
reducing bright 49
sensitivity to 60
lining up objects 46
local newspaper, contact
your 108
locker rooms and
swimming 129–30
looking away, constant 60

lost, what to do when
123–6

manipulating autistic
people to commit
crime 70–1
Maryland Police and
Correctional Training
Commission 21
medication, administering
77
mental illness, autistic
behavior resembling
symptoms of 41
calling law enforcement
because of 46
mental retardation 14, 20
"Mike, Mr" vi
mimicking 36
monotonous voice 60
motor skills 29–30
movie theaters 134–8

National Autism Society
61
National Information
Center for Children
and Youth with
Disabilities
(NICCHY) 108
National Victim Assistance
Academy report
(1999) 20, 21
neck or face, do not touch
61
neighbors 101
noise
breaking object as
response to 37

inappropriate response to 32, 37–8
reducing loud 49
non-response does not imply guilt 50
nonverbal and non-responsive to verbal cues 28–9, 36, 60

obsessive recitations of information 53, 61
odors
  protective responses to 62
  reducing 49
object spinning and preference for repetitive motion 27
obliviousness to emotions 31–2, 37
odd behaviors, don't interpret as belligerent 52–3
Odenwalt, Sr., Sergeant David P. 44–5
Office for Victims of Crime, US Department of Justice 20
order and routine 30–1, 37
over-stimulation 34
  avoid in emergency room situation 81

pain 34
  insensitivity to 25, 35
  interpretation may be abnormal 80

parents
how emergency responders can work together with 95–113
  carry autism emergency ID card 98–9
  carry law enforcement pocket cards 109–10
  contact your local newspaper 108
  educate yourself and get involved 108–9
  give educational presentations 107–8
  give training sessions 104–6
  give your child a form of communication 100–1
  have your child wear emergency ID tag 99–100
  hold an awareness day 102–3
  install screen doors and alarms 97–8
  instructional message to parents 96–113
  introduce your child in public places you frequent 102

  knock on your neighbors' doors 101
  make political contacts 109
  register your child 104
  safety-proof your home 97
  teach safety procedures to your child 110–12
  use emergency alert decals 98
  use social stories 112–13
restraining children suspected of abuse 44–5, 46
passivity, extreme, or hyperactivity 27–8, 36
PECS (Picture Exchange Communication) 54, 100
peering into windows, calling law enforcement because of 40–1, 45
Penn, Dr vi
personal space, poor judgment of 57, 61
physical abuse 21
pica (eating inappropriate objects, e.g. rocks, mud, glass) 46
picture cards 53, 62, 96
pinching, self- 45
Plano, Texas 11
pointing 31

avoid 61
Police Executive Research
    Forum (PERF) 21
police 18, 20
    register autistic child
        with, in emergency
        48
    see also law enforcement
political contacts, making
    109
ponds, lakes and pools,
    wandering alone into
    45
predicting reactions,
    difficulty in 61
preventing problems in
    everyday life 115–38
    bathrooms and lavatories
        128–9
    entrance and exits
        126–8
    locker rooms and
        swimming 129–30
    movie theaters 134–8
    restaurants 130–1
    social awareness and
        safety when shopping
        119–23
    street safety 117–19
    telephone and 911 (999)
        use 115–17
    travel 131–3
    what to do when lost
        123–6
private parts, touching of
    57, 61
public crisis situations,
    handling 134–8

public places you frequent,
    introduce your child
    in 102
problems, difficulty in
    distinguishing
    between minor and
    serious 61
public lavatories 128–9
punching 34
    -self 45

Qualls, the vi

Rain Man 19
rapid movement and
    pointing, avoid 61
recitations of information,
    obsessive 53, 61
register autistic child
    on all emergency service
        data banks 104
    with police in
        emergency 48
repeat requests calmly and
    softly 61
repeat short, direct phrases
    50
repetitive actions/motion
    do not stop unless
        self-injurious 62
    preference for 27, 35–6
        calling law
            enforcement
            because of 45
responses, common autistic
    57–9
restaurants 130–1
restraint 68, 70
retailers, problems for
    89–94

Reynolds, Shelley vi, 86
rights, understanding 62
robotic-like speech and
    movements 19, 36,
    42, 46, 56–7
rocking, head or body 34,
    45
routine
    and order 30–1, 37
    traffic stops 71–2
running away 60

safety 18, 19
    how to make travel
        communications
        safety book 147–9
    procedures to your child,
        teaching 110–12
    -proof your home 97
    social stories 157–68
        fire at Chris's
            house 161–2
        going to autism
            rally in D.C.
            166–8
        meeting Officer
            Chris 164–5
        riding in car 163
        travel and,
            communication
            car book
            152–6
        what I do when I
            hear the fire
            alarm in my
            home 160
        when I am hurt in
            accident 157–9
    street 117–19

when shopping and
social awareness
119–23
savants 14
scratching 34
self- 45
screen doors and alarms,
install 97 8
security blanket 30
seizure(s) 14
disorders, be aware of
62
self-absorption 13
self-biting 34, 45
self-education 108–9
self-help skills, weak 61
Self-injurious/
self-stimulatory
behavior 24, 34, 60
calling law enforcement
because of 39–40, 45
self-injury 14
self-pinching 45
self-punching 45
self-scratching 45
sensitivity to stimuli 60
September 11 2001
tragedy 134
severe learning disabilities
20
sexual abuse 21
sharp objects, lack of
understanding of 38
shoplifting and store
disturbances 89–94
overview 93–4
shopping, safety during
and social awareness
119–23

short phrases and direct
language, using 52,
61
sign language 36
smell(s)
protective responses to
62
reducing 49
sensitivity to 60
Smithgau, Mayor vi
social awareness and safety
when shopping
119–23
social cues, inability to
understand 60
socialization techniques,
lack of 37
social stories 112–13
safety 157–68
soft gestures 52
sound(s)
protective responses to
62
reducing loud 49
sensitivity to 60
spinning 45
objects 27, 34, 35–6
self 34
spit, playing with 60
spitting 57, 60
standing too close 61
avoidance of 62
staring 57
stims 24
stimulants, reducing 49
stomach disorders 14
strangers, may willingly go
with 38
street safety 117–19
surprise 34

aversion to 35
suspected drug abuse or
mental illness, calling
law enforcement
because of 41
Susquehanna Valley
Emergency Medical
Services (EMS) 79
swimming and locker
rooms 129–30
symptoms of autism
at age two 12–13,
23–38
overview 34–8

tact, lack of 55–6
taking into custody 69–70
tapping, head 34
teaching
methods, unresponsive
to normal 27, 35
safety procedures to your
child 110–12
teasing, inability to
understand 60
telephone and 911 (999)
use 115–17
temperatures
protective responses to
62
sensitivity to 60
Texas Commission on Law
Enforcement Officer
Training and
Education 21
textures, sensitivity to 60
theft and autism 91–2
thrashing 45
self 67
timeliness, obsessive 37

toe walking 42, 46
touch
    aversion to 26, 35
    protective responses to
        62
traffic, running into 38, 45
training
    sessions 104–6
    need for 17–22
transfixing on objects 34
travel 131–3
    communications safety
        book, how to make
        147–9
    safety social stories
        riding in car 163
        travel and safety
            communication
            car book
            152–6
turning on and off water
    faucets (taps)
    repetitively 41, 45

"Unlocking Autism" 86
unresponsive to normal
    teaching methods 27,
    35
US Court of Appeals Tenth
    Circuit 21
US Department of Justice
    20
using others as tool to get
    what you want 31, 37

verbal commands,
    non-response to 38
verbal cues, nonverbal and
    non-responsive to
    28–9, 36

vestibular problems 29
violence 14, 25
volume, poor judge of 60
vomiting 35

Walk in the Mall, A vii–ix
wandering alone 40
    calling law enforcement
        because of 45
    into ponds, lakes and
        pools 45
Warkomski, Dr Fran vi
Washington, Doris vi
water, attraction to 45
water faucets (taps),
        turning on and off
        repetitively 41, 45
what is autism? 11–15
windows, peering into
    40–1, 45
World Trade Center
    disaster 134–5
Wossidlo, Lenore P. vi, 96
wraparound method of
    restraint 68–9

yes/no
    responses to questions
        60
    signboards 62